Beginning Digital Image Processing

Using Free Tools for Photographers

Sebastian Montabone

Apress®

Beginning Digital Image Processing: Using Free Tools for Photographers

ISBN-13 (pbk): 978-1-4302-2841-7

ISBN-13 (electronic): 978-1-4302-2842-4

Printed and bound in the United States of America 9 8 7 6 5 4 3 2 1

President and Publisher: Paul Manning
Lead Editor: Frank Pohlmann, Brian MacDonald
Technical Reviewer: Roger Wickes
Editorial Board: Clay Andres, Steve Anglin, Mark Beckner, Ewan Buckingham, Gary Cornell, Jonathan Gennick, Jonathan Hassell, Michelle Lowman, Matthew Moodie, Duncan Parkes, Jeffrey Pepper, Frank Pohlmann, Douglas Pundick, Ben Renow-Clarke, Dominic Shakeshaft, Matt Wade, Tom Welsh
Coordinating Editor: Jim Markham
Copy Editor: Ralph Moore
Compositor: Bytheway Publishing Services
Indexer: Brenda Miller
Cover Designer: Anna Ishchenko

Distributed to the book trade worldwide by Springer Science+Business Media, LLC., 233 Spring Street, 6th Floor, New York, NY 10013. Phone 1-800-SPRINGER, fax (201) 348-4505, e-mail orders-ny@springer-sbm.com, or visit www.springeronline.com.

For information on translations, please e-mail rights@apress.com, or visit www.apress.com.

Apress and friends of ED books may be purchased in bulk for academic, corporate, or promotional use. eBook versions and licenses are also available for most titles. For more information, reference our Special Bulk Sales–eBook Licensing web page at www.apress.com/info/bulksales.

The source code for this book is available to readers at www.apress.com. You will need to answer questions pertaining to this book in order to successfully download the code.

To my lovely Sarah.

Contents at a Glance

Contents

About the Author

■ **Sebastian Montabone** is a computer engineer with a Master of Science degree in computer vision. After publishing his thesis on human detection in unconstrained environments, he has worked in different areas such as intelligent IP cameras for automated surveillance, data mining, game development, and embedded devices. Currently he is a software consultant and entrepreneur.

About the Technical Reviewer

■ **Roger Wickes** has been involved with software for over 30 years, having had the privilege of participating in the monumental convergences that have shaped computing in all of its dimensions. He started his career learning leadership at Admiral Farragut and the USCG Academy, and fell in love with computerized simulation. His first commercial job was working for CSC at the Naval Underwater Systems Center on big secret underwater things. He then learned how to consult and worked in an entrepreneurial environment for Technology Applications and Development Company in Newport, RI. Tired of the snow, he joined the Fortune 100 company EDS (now HP) in Georgia, where he learned structured techniques for software development, the financials of running a large business, global consulting, and all the leadership skills needed to operate the Atlanta Service Center of 120 professionals developing software on all the major platforms. Sensing the opportunity of the Internet and Web, he was a founding partner in ITG, filling all roles from Consultant, Account Manager, and CFO. At ITG, he was promoted to CIO, where he enabled and led the development of the first Internet-based payroll and staff exchange systems. He fell in love with visual imagery and Blender a decade ago, is a Blender Certified Instructor, consultant, and author of *Blender Essentials* by Lynda.com and *Foundation Blender Compositing* by Apress. He has been the animator for TV commercials, games, and film. He enjoys scuba diving, skiing, travel, and enabling the next gen. His web site is rogerwickes.com.

Acknowledgments

I would like to thank the developers of the many tools described in this book, which I have been using for years.

First of all, many thanks to the developers of GIMP for creating excellent software for general image editing. The developers of ImageMagick deserve a big thank you for their incredible work making the most powerful command-line image-processing program. The people behind the Hugin project deserve great thanks for making the creation of panoramas a joy. I would also like to express my gratitude to the developers of Qtpfsgui for making HDR imaging easy. Thanks to all of those behind the UFRaw project for allowing us to read many RAW formats as well as to the developers of Avidemux for creating a simple and useful video editor. Special thanks to Dr. Paul Harrison, the developer of the excellent Resyntheziser GIMP plug-in and Phil Harvey, for creating the best tool for dealing with metadata: ExifTool. This book could not exist without all of your amazing work.

Last but not least, I would very much like to thank the staff at Apress for assisting in editing this book. It has been a lot of work and their input has been invaluable in enhancing the content of this book.

Introduction

Digital image post-processing and open-source software are exciting topics; this book is the fusion of both. How cool is that? After you read this book, you will be able to edit your images for free.

This book starts with some background information about photography and digital images to give the reader a common base. Then, several image post-processing techniques are presented with ascending difficulty, from simple resizing or cropping to more advanced subjects such as high dynamic range (HDR) imaging, distortion correction, or panoramas. Armed with these techniques, using the best open-source tools available, you will be ready to start editing your images for free. In each case, I will show you the best free tools for the job. Finally, as an added bonus, the last two chapters cover extra stuff: video processing for creating your own movies from single video clips and CHDK to enhance your camera features.

The first chapter of the book introduces general photography concepts. You will learn common concepts used in photography so that you can control your camera to take the shots that you want. Understanding these concepts is the key to shooting a good photo, which in turn is the starting point for image editing.

The second chapter describes all the details of digital images. Because you are going to work with digital images, in-depth knowledge is beneficial before you start editing.

The third chapter covers the simplest and most common post-processing techniques. Every photographer often needs to resize or crop their images so that they fit in the specific medium they want to present. All these operations and more are presented in this chapter.

The fourth chapter explains how to control color in your images. Everything that you need to know is here. The fifth chapter covers the most commonly used filters in digital photography, such as noise reduction, blur, or the unsharp mask. The sixth chapter covers the photo retouching techniques that photographers use to fix images with small problems such as skin blemishes, removing small objects, and so forth.

Chapter 7 covers a more advanced technique, HDR. You will learn how to create those images from ordinary pictures. Chapter 8 covers distortion correction. It shows you how to correct the distortion produced by perspective and lenses. In Chapter 9, you will understand how to take the images needed for making panoramas as well as how to create them.

The last two chapters cover bonus material. Chapter 10 teaches you how to create movies from your video clips, and Chapter 11 describes how to use CHDK to enhance your camera's features.

I hope you enjoy this journey into open-source digital-image post-processing!

CHAPTER 1

■ ■ ■

Digital Photography

Have you ever wanted to make panoramic photos like the one shown in Figure 1-1?

Figure 1-1. *You can take panoramas like this.*

How about fix the perspective distortion when you shoot a building, as in Figure 1-2?

 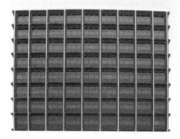

Figure 1-2. *Or perspective shots.*

Or simply remove a complete object from your photograph, as in Figure 1-3?

Figure 1-3. *Or do some magic.*

In this book, I will explain how to do these things and more with the help of free software—you don't have to buy expensive software to achieve these results. After you finish reading this book, you will be able to convert your images into great-looking photos using the software and techniques I describe.

But let's go one step at a time. There are some things you have to understand first so that you can get the best results for your photos. Let's start with what digital photography actually is.

In its most general sense, photography is the process of generating a two-dimensional view of a three-dimensional space using light. In simpler terms, photography is the art of drawing with light.

Light and Photography

Light comes from many different sources. Some of these are natural, such as the sun, lightning, fire, or even glowworms. Other sources are not commonly found in nature, such as halogen lamps, incandescent light bulbs, neon lights, or light-emitting diodes.

As light travels through the air, or any other substance such as water or even vacuum, it usually runs into objects. When this happens, some part of the light gets absorbed by the object and some of it gets reflected. This reflection allows us to see objects that do not emit their own light, which are the most common ones in our world.

Humans are able to see objects because of our extraordinary visual system, which is composed of the eyes and some parts of the brain. The eyes gather light from the current field of view, forming an image in the retina. This information is processed by the brain, producing the visual perception of the world that we know. By changing the position of our eyes, we can select the field of view that we want to look at.

In photography, the light from the current field of view of the camera is projected on a photographic film or an electronic sensor, producing an image. This idea is based on the camera obscura (Latin for dark chamber) and it is where the name *camera* comes from.

The camera obscura is an old invention that consists in a closed room (or box) that has only one small hole or aperture on the exterior of one of the sides. Because light generally travels in straight lines, the light from the exterior passes through the aperture and gets projected upside-down into the opposite side, preserving its color and perspective. Figure 1-4 shows how this works.

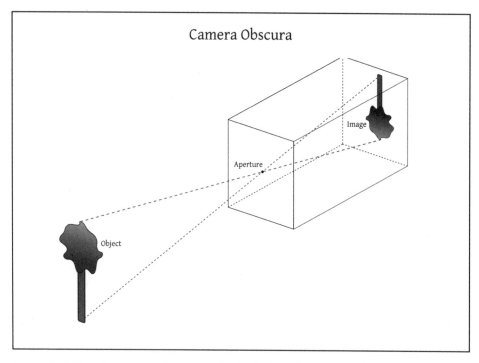

Figure 1-4. How the camera obscura works. Light from the exterior of the room passes through the small aperture and gets projected into the opposite wall, inverted.

Some of the users of the camera obscura were astronomers and artists. Astronomers could see the movement of the sun without damaging their eyes, and artists could place a translucent screen and trace the outlines obtaining realistic paintings. This was the start of rotoscoping as a technique used in film and media.

The field of view that gets projected into the screen depends on the distance from the screen to the aperture. In photography, this distance is similar to the concept of focal length. Because the screen remains the same size, an image created by a large field of view presents smaller objects than an image produced by a small field of view (see Figure 1-5). This is similar in the human eye. The field of view that you see is given by the distance from your pupil to the retina. It also depends on other things; for example, you have a larger field of view when viewing with your two eyes instead of just one because of the processing done in the brain.

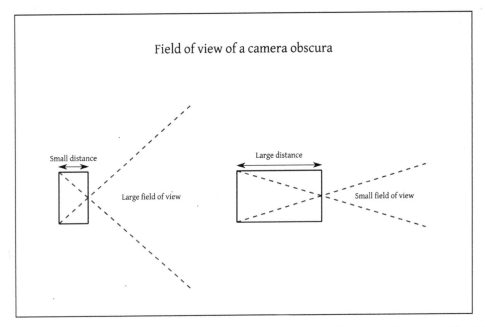

Figure 1-5. The relationship between the distance of the sides of a camera obscura and its field of view. Larger distances produce narrower fields of view (think of zoomed in). Smaller distances produce larger fields of view (think of zoomed out).

The main problem with the camera obscura is that the resulting image is very dim because of the small amount of light that passes through the aperture. To solve the problem, Giambattista Della Porta started using converging lenses. The result of this is that the rays of light are projected into a smaller image; therefore, more brightness is achieved, obtaining better projections.

Advances in chemistry allowed storing the projected images permanently. At first, photographic plates were used, but later they were replaced by photographic film, which has evolved into what is being used in modern film cameras. The standard photographic film format is the 135 film, which is commonly known as 35mm because of its width. When digital cameras refer to having a full-frame sensor, it means that its size is the same as the 35mm film frame, which is 24x36mm (see Figure 1-6).

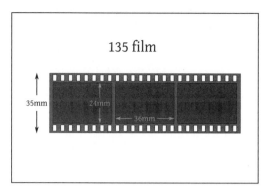

Figure 1-6. *The dimensions of the commonly used 135 film. The standard size of each frame is 24mm x 36mm. The perforations on the sides are used to move the film. Each frame contains exactly eight perforations on each side so that the camera can move the film correctly to the next frame.*

The introduction of a medium to store light gave birth to photography. Image quality of the photographs started to improve year after year, adding more details and color. The process of developing photographs was also improved. All of these made taking photographs much easier, making it very popular among the public.

For many years, film cameras were the standard. Usually, a person would take up to 36 photographs (depending on the length of the film) with their camera and then send the film to a lab for developing. Expert photographers would develop their own photographs, having total control on the final image. This development is a chemical process done in a dark room that transfers the information from the film onto photographic paper. How this developing process is done, which specific photographic paper is used, and other factors influence in how the resulting photograph will look.

Advances in electronics resulted in the invention of the charged coupled device (CCD), which in conjunction with other technologes led to the origin of digital photography.

Digital photography uses electronic components to capture and store light instead of film. Digital cameras started to be produced and consumed by many people. Although at the beginning, the image quality was very poor, today's digital cameras produce images comparable to film cameras.

The main components of a digital camera are the lens, the viewfinder or LCD screen, the CCD, the image storing device, and the shutter button, along with the different controls available in the camera.

You should select your camera components based on what you are planning to photograph. The perfect camera for taking pictures of your friends at a party may be very different from the perfect camera for taking pictures of landscapes. Because the selection of your camera components is very important, let's examine these components in more detail.

Digital Camera

You probably grew up with cameras in the house, and the basic principles are simple enough that even a child can understand them: point and shoot. Digital cameras are a different animal than the film cameras you probably had as a kid, and they're evolving rapidly. Some parts are still easily recognizable from film cameras, such as the lens and shutter control, but other parts are unique to digital cameras, such as the LCD screen and the sensor. Knowing your camera is an important first step to taking good photos, so I'm going to go over the components in this section. Although each brand and model of camera has small differences, there are enough similarities that you should be able to apply this discussion to your specific camera.

Lens

The lens is the surface of entry of the light into the camera. It is responsible for directing the light from outside the camera to the sensor, where the image is created. Assuming that the camera is always in the same physical position, the specific field of view that the camera is looking at, which is what will be shown in the picture, is defined by the focal length of the lens. The *focal length* is the distance from the lens to the point where all the incoming rays of light converge due to the optics of the lens. Similar to the camera obscura, a lens with a small focal length produces an image with a large angle of view, while on the other hand a lens with a large focal length produces an image with a small angle of view.

Some lenses have the ability to change the focal length in a specific range, like the one in Figure 1-7. This is commonly known as *optical zoom*. When the photographer zooms in, he sees that the objects appear larger. This is because he is increasing the focal length of the lens. When zooming out, he is decreasing the focal length of the lens, causing the objects to appear smaller.

Figure 1-7. This image shows a digital single lens reflex camera with a lens mounted. This particular lens allows changing the focal length from 18 to 55 mm. The currently selected focal length is 35 mm.

Note that optical zoom is different than *digital zoom*. Optical zoom means that the optics of the camera are changed so a different field of view will be captured. Digital zoom is a quick resize and crop operation done inside the camera on the original field of view. Due to the limited processing power and time available in the camera, the result is not always acceptable. You can always achieve the same or better results afterwards in the post processing stage so I strongly recommend that you don't use the digital zoom feature on the camera itself.

Newer models of camera lenses offer a very useful feature called Image Stabilization (IS) or Vibration Reduction (VR). This feature compensates the camera shakes made by the hand of the photographer, allowing you to take sharper photographs without a tripod. It is a complex system that reads information from sensors, accelerometers, and gyroscopes, and moves the lens elements accordingly to compensate the movement of the camera in real time. If you are planning to buy a new lens, I highly recommend you buy one that has this feature; it will make your photographs look much sharper.

Viewfinder or LCD Screen

The viewfinder is the part of the camera that allows you to observe the scene that is going to be photographed. Some cameras offer an LCD screen to observe the scene as well, but there is a difference between them depending on the camera type and model.

In digital single lens reflex cameras (DSLR), like the one shown in Figure 1-8, the viewfinder is connected directly to the light coming from the lens using reflection of an internal mirror. When the photograph is taken, the internal mirror moves to direct the light into the sensor instead of into the viewfinder. This movement is the cause of the typical noise of the DSLRs when taking a photograph. Also, because of this design, the LCD screen in most old DSLRs cannot show the so-called live preview because the light is always being directed only to the viewfinder. Newer models of DSLR have solved this problem by adding a second sensor dedicated only to the live preview and complex mirroring systems.

Figure 1-8. *The back of a DSLR. You can see both the viewfinder (above) and the LCD screen (below) from this view.*

In point-and-shoot digital cameras, there is a separate small lens located in a specific position, usually above the main lens, for directing the light to the viewfinder. This provides a rough estimate of the scene, but should not be used for serious photographs. Because the location of the small lens is different than the main lens, the actual photograph will have a different field of view than the image seen in the viewfinder. The LCD screen, on the other hand, is always showing the image represented by the light coming from the main lens to the sensor. When using point-and-shoot digital cameras, I recommend that you mostly use the LCD screen for composing the photograph and only use the viewfinder in bright sunlight. Actually, some camera manufacturing companies have opted for not including the viewfinder in new, smaller models.

If you own a camera with a viewfinder and an LCD screen, and both read the information from the main lens, it is a matter of taste as to which one to use, as both of them present advantages and disadvantages. For example, the LCD screen can be useless in a very bright location. When you use the viewfinder, your head needs to be physically close to the camera, which in some cases may be impossible or uncomfortable. On the other hand, LCD screens can be useful for displaying extra information, such as marking over or underexposed areas so that you can make sure your photo will be properly exposed when you take it. Finally, viewfinders show exactly the same light that will be used to generate the photograph, without any processing of the sensor, therefore showing more accurate information.

Sensor

The camera sensor is where the light is converted into an electric signal. The input to the sensor is light and the output is an array of voltages, one for each pixel location. Further processing is needed to generate the image from this array of voltages, which can be done in the camera itself or later in a computer.

To generate the array of voltages, the sensor has a fixed number of many small light sensors, one for each pixel, that sense the light when the photograph is taken. During the exposure, all these small light sensors start receiving light and when the exposure is finished, they stop receiving light and store the amount of voltage generated. More light received means more voltage measured by these small light sensors.

To create the image, the voltage stored on each small light sensor is compared to their possible range of voltage, which is called *dynamic range*. If there were no light coming in, the output for that specific position of the image would be considered black, and if the amount of received light produces more or the same voltage than the defined maximum of the small light sensor, the output for that specific position of the image would be considered white.

Voltage values inside the range of every small light sensor would produce different grayscale values in the image. Therefore, sensors with a larger dynamic range can sense a larger range of different light intensities in the same shot. In other words, there would be less overexposed or underexposed areas in a sensor with a larger dynamic range than in one with a small dynamic range given the same light as input.

The previous method explains how to capture the intensity of the incoming light, producing grayscale images. In order to produce a color image, a little more needs to be done.

All the visible colors can be decomposed as functions of three primary colors: red, green, and blue. For example, if you mix red and green in equal proportions, yellow is generated. Therefore, to produce color images, one can use three of these arrays of small light sensors with a filter for each of the red, green, and blue and then combine their results.

This design is expensive, though, and almost every digital camera uses a different approach: The Bayer filter. This approach uses only one array but every small light sensor has a filter so it can only sense one specific color: red, green, or blue. The camera, or the computer, can then process this **RAW** (or unprocessed) data to form the final image.

The megapixel (MP) count of a sensor tells you the number of small sensors it has, and also the number of pixels of the image it produces. A higher MP count gives you better-quality images, but it also means that your images file sizes will be larger, which means that you will have room for less pictures on your memory card.

Storage

The storage component allows you to save the images in a permanent way; you can access them later from a computer or any other device. Normally a memory card is used for storage in most digital cameras.

There are different types of memory cards: Multi Media Cards (MMC), Secure Digital (SD), xD Picture Cards (xD), Compact Flash (CF), and Sony Memory Sticks (MS). All of them have similar performance, but each camera can only use the memory card it was designed to use (some cameras can read more than one format). Currently, the most widely used type is the SD memory card shown in Figure 1-9, so if you have to make a choice, it would be better to buy a camera that can support this technology, as it is turning into the standard.

Figure 1-9. This picture shows three SD cards with different storage sizes and brand names.

The main features that you should look for when buying a new memory card are the storage capacity and the writing speed. I would recommend that you buy a memory card with at least 1 or 2 GB of storage capacity, which will give you plenty of space for storing your images. As prices are constantly going down, I recommend that you buy the memory card with the largest capacity available for the specific camera that you own. Remember that an image with a higher megapixel (MP) count will end up using more space in the card, and that RAW data consumes much more space than the processed JPEG image.

About writing speed, it is better to buy a fast card because it will minimize the time between two shots. This is especially useful when taking photographs in continuous mode or when making videos where continuous writing to the card is made. Look for memory cards with 150x or faster writing speed to get the best results.

Controls

The controls of the camera allow you to define how and when the photograph is going to be taken. All digital cameras provide you with a shutter button, which is the responsible for initiating the process of creating the photograph. Before taking the photograph, you can adjust the specific settings for the shot.

Some point-and-shoot digital cameras only offer automatic settings, which means that the photographer only can access the shutter button and all the settings are calculated by the camera itself. Other models offer a mixture between fully automatic and manual mode, which means the photographer can specify different settings.

In DSLRs, the photographer can define all of the settings. The main difference in controls between DSLR models is that smaller cameras do not have physical knobs for changing the settings; therefore, the photographer needs to rely on the LCD screen to adjust them. On larger cameras, the photographer can change the controls using physical knobs, making it easier for her to change the settings while taking a photograph.

As always, there is a compromise with every added feature; therefore, selecting which camera is better for you will depend on how you plan to use it. The larger the camera, the better controls and quality it will have, but at the cost of being heavier, less portable, and more expensive.

Creating a Photograph

The entire process of taking a photograph involves three steps, shown in Figure 1-10. The first step is to define the specific view of the real world that is going to be photographed, which is called *composition*. This is obtained by changing the focal length of the lens, commonly known as zoom, or by changing the positioning or orientation of the camera itself until the desired scene is presented in the viewfinder.

The second step is to gather just enough light from the selected field of view to capture the desired photograph. The total amount of light gathered in the process of taking the photograph is called *exposure*. If not enough light is gathered, the image is said to be *underexposed* and it will look too dark or black. On the other hand, if there is more than just the needed light, the image is said to be *overexposed* and it will look too bright or white. The correct exposure is achieved using a combination of three controls: shutter speed, aperture, and sensitivity, which are described later.

The third and final step is called *post-processing*. In film, this step is done in a dark room and only professionals can do it, so most of us need to send the photos to a lab and wait for the final images. In digital photography, the post-production is done on the computer. This means that you don't need to send your photos to another person; you can process your own images yourself. In this step, the photographer produces the final image, correcting mistakes done in the previous two steps, adjusting the colors, applying filters, and in general making all the necessary changes needed for producing a great-looking photograph using image processing tools.

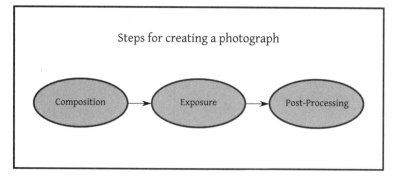

Figure 1-10. Three steps to create a photograph.

Composition

Composition relates to selecting the right field of view at the right time to create a good-looking picture. Creating great compositions is more of an art than a science. A good composition is made of an interesting subject with the correct lightning and presented in a good background and perspective. There are many books that you can read about these topics, but I will give you some basic guidelines that can be useful when taking pictures.

Field of View

The field of view defines exactly which objects are going to be present in the photograph and the perspective. You can change the field of view by changing the focal length of the lens and also by moving or rotating the camera. Changing the focal length of the lens does not change the perspective in the photograph; it only enlarges the central area of the image, maintaining the relative sizes of the objects. On the other hand, changing the position of the camera changes the perspective. This means that closer objects will look larger than objects that are farther away.

To make these concepts clear, I will show you the effect of each of them in a real-world example. Figure 1-11 shows an idea of the layout of the real-world objects used in this example. The larger cone will be the foreground object, the small cone will be in the background in the left side of the image, and the trees will appear far behind in the background.

Figure 1-11. The layout of the objects in the real-world example

First, I will show you the effect of changing the focal length of the lens without moving the camera. Figures 1-12 through 1-14 show that larger focal lengths produce narrower fields of view and smaller focal lengths produce deeper fields of view (the same concept as in the camera obscura). The effect is that the center area of the image gets enlarged, but the perspective remains the same. The size of the objects in the foreground is changed in the same proportion as the size of the objects in the background. Note how the cones and the trees maintain the distance between them, changing their image size on each picture.

Figure 1-12. *This picture was taken with a focal length of 6mm. Note how far apart the cones and trees look at this focal length; you can see a large field of view.*

Figure 1-13. *This picture was taken with a focal length of 10mm. Note how increasing the focal length reduces the field of view. If you compare this image to the previous one, the center of the image got enlarged and the objects at the borders are no longer present.*

Figure 1-14. This picture was taken with a focal length of 35mm. Note how close the cones look now and how reduced the field of view is. Also, the perspective and relative sizes of the objects remained constant in all these images.

The second point I want to show you is how the field of view changes when moving the camera while maintaining the focal length of the lens constant. When moving the camera to another location, a change in perspective is achieved. Figures 1-15 through 1-17 show the same scene viewed from different locations, keeping the focal length constant. Note how now the distance between the objects as well as their size change from picture to picture.

Figure 1-15. *This picture was taken at roughly 15 meters from the object. Notice the relative sizes of the objects at this distance. The cones seem much smaller than the tree behind them. Also, it seems that the two cones and the tree are close.*

Figure 1-16. *This picture was taken at roughly 6 meters from the object. Notice how now the cones appear larger than before, compared to the tree behind them. We can also see that the distances between the objects have increased.*

Figure 1-17. This picture was taken at roughly 2 meters from the object. At this distance, the first cone appears as large as the tree. Also, the distances between the objects seem much larger than before.

You can obtain an interesting effect by changing the focal length and location of the camera so that the target object fills the same area in the viewfinder on each image. In Figures 1-18 through 1-21, note how the foreground object remains roughly the same size and position while the background gets larger on each picture. The effect is more noticeable when the objects are far away like the trees in this example. Using this technique, you can change how the background will appear in the scene without changing the size of the foreground object. In general, a large focal length presents a flat image, whereas a small focal length shows the objects more separated in the image. Because of this, when photographing a portrait, it is a good idea to get very close to the person and shoot with a small focal length, so that the face can stand out from the background.

Figure 1-18. This picture was taken with a focal length of 6mm.

Figure 1-19. *This picture was taken with a focal length of 10mm.*

Figure 1-20. *This picture was taken with a focal length of 13mm.*

Figure 1-21. This picture was taken with a focal length of 20mm.

Composition Rules

One of the most well-known rules for composing in photography is the *rule of thirds*. It says that the photographer should visualize the image divided by three vertical and horizontal lines. The most important aspects of the image should be placed along these lines or in the intersection of them. This rule is particularly useful when taking photographs of landscapes where the horizon is usually placed near one of the horizontal lines covering one- or two-thirds of the image, as in Figure 1-22. Placing the objects of interest using this rule produces more balanced and interesting photographs than centering the objects. This rule is based on the idea that the center of attention of humans is around those areas.

Figure 1-22. This image shows an example of the usage of the rule of thirds.

Another rule to take into account is *symmetry*. This rule tells you that you should try to put similar elements on both sides of the image so that the image is balanced. Also, you can put similar objects at the top and at the bottom of your image. This way, you can create vertical or horizontal symmetry. Similar to the rule of thirds where objects of interest were not placed in the center, you may break the symmetry of a view to create interesting photographs.

Background clutter can ruin a photograph, so try to isolate your object of interest as much as possible. You can use focal length and aperture to separate and blur the background. If background clutter is impossible to avoid, try creating a natural frame in the scene using the background. This can help in generating an interesting photograph.

Note that these rules are just a rough guideline to composition and that there are many more techniques that professional photographers use. Also, once you know all the rules, you can start breaking them, but for beginners they are a good rule of thumb.

Exposure

Exposure is the total amount of light that gets into the sensor. Digital cameras normally have the shutter closed, so that no light gets inside the camera. Once you press the button to take the photograph, the shutter opens up to a certain size, which is called *aperture*, and remains open until a certain time has passed, which is called *shutter speed* or *exposure time*. Inside the camera, the sensor awaits the incoming light with a predefined *sensitivity*. With these three controls, you can tell the camera how much light you want to capture. If you capture too much light, your photo will be entirely white, and if you don't capture enough light, your image will be black. Also, each control affects how the image will look if you change it. I will describe now these three controls, starting with shutter speed because it is the simpler to understand.

Shutter Speed

The term *shutter speed* refers to the amount of time that the camera gathers light. It is measured in seconds or fractions of seconds. It is also known as exposure time and it is represented by the symbol Tv. Some standard values are: 1/60, 1/30, 1/15, 1/8, 1/4, 1/2, 1". These numbers were specifically defined so that for every step increased in the exposure time, the amount of light gathered, or exposure, is doubled. On the other hand, if the exposure time is decreased by one step, the exposure of the photograph is halved. You can also use any number in between these values. In other words, the amount of light that goes into the sensor is proportional to the amount of time that the shutter is open. For example, if the current exposure time is set to 1/15 and the photographer changes the shutter speed to 1/30, the amount of light received by the sensor will be half of what was before because the exposure time would be shorter. Figures 1-23 and 1-24 show this effect.

By changing the shutter speed, the photographer can control how the movement of the objects will be perceived in the photograph. For example, water moving on a river can be presented very smoothly if a long exposure time is selected, for example 1". On the other hand, water can be presented sharp if the shutter speed is faster, such as 1/60, which is one sixth of a second of exposure time. If you want to freeze a moving object, you need to set the shutter speed to a value similar to the object speed. If you want to show the object moving, you need to select a slower shutter speed. The disadvantage of using long exposure times is that the camera has to be perfectly still or the photograph will come out blurred. You can use tripods or flat surfaces to keep the camera as still as possible. This partially solves the problem, but your finger slightly moves the camera when you push the shutter button. One suggestion to avoid this is to use the self timer setting of the camera; set this timer to about two seconds. Using this technique, the camera will itself take the photograph two seconds after you press the shutter button, remaining still while the exposure is being done.

Figure 1-23. *This picture was taken with shutter speed of 1/100s. Note how some drops of water are visible.*

Figure 1-24. This picture was taken with a shutter speed of 1/20 s. Note how the water looks blurred because of the slower shutter speed.

Aperture

The *aperture* control allows you to change the size of the aperture where the light enters into the sensor. It is represented by the symbol Av and it is measured in F-numbers. An F-number is the focal length of the lens divided by the diameter of the actual aperture. Because of this, having the focal length constant, larger apertures represent smaller F-numbers and smaller apertures represent larger F-numbers. Some standard F-numbers are F1.4, F2, F2.8, F4.0, F5.6, F8.0 (another common notation for F-numbers is f/X, for example, f/1.4, having the same meaning as F1.4). These numbers were defined so that every step increased in the F-number halves the exposure. On the other hand, every step decreased in the F-number doubles the exposure. For example, if the current F-number is F2.8 and the photographer changes the aperture to F2, the amount of light received by the sensor will be double of what it was before because the aperture would be larger. You can combine your changes in aperture with exposure time so that the exposure remains the same. This means, for example, that F2.8 at 1/30" will gather the same amount of light that F2 at 1/60" would. This way, you can control the effect you want in the photograph without over- or underexposing it. First, get the correct exposure for your photograph and then you can increase or decrease a control, compensating with another one.

Changing the aperture allows the photographer to select how much of the image is in focus, which is called the depth of field. For example, in a portrait, it is generally required that only the face of the person is in focus, while all the background is blurred. This can be obtained by selecting a large aperture (small F-number) such as F1.4. Figures 1-25 and 1-26 show this effect. On the other hand, a landscape would require that everything looks focused; therefore a small aperture (large F-number) such as F8.0 should be used in that case.

Figure 1-25. A small aperture (large F-number) of F8.0 was used in this picture. Note how both the background and the foreground are in focus.

Figure 1-26. A large aperture (small F-number) of F2.8 was used in this picture. Note how the background is blurred but the foreground is in focus.

Sensitivity

The *sensitivity* control defines how sensitive the sensor will be to the incoming light. It is represented by an ISO rating. Some standard values are 100, 200, 400, and 800. A sensitivity of 100 is the normal value. Increasing the sensitivity in one step allows the photographer to achieve a proper exposure with half of the previously needed light. This means that by increasing the sensitivity, you can take photographs in lower lighting conditions, or with a smaller aperture (larger F-number), or with a shorter exposure time.

Although the idea of increasing the sensitivity sounds good, it has some disadvantages. When increasing the sensitivity, the signal coming from the sensor gets amplified. This also means that the original *noise* of the sensor gets amplified too. Noise in digital images can be seen as randomly placed pixels of different colors. Noise degrades notably the quality of the image and should be avoided as much as possible. In Figure 1-27, you can see the same objects photographed with equal conditions, only changing the ISO setting from 80 to 800. You can see how for this particular sensor the noise level is nonexistent in ISO 80 and very high when the ISO is set to 800.

Figure 1-27. The left shot was made with ISO 800. Note how grainy the image looks. This is caused by the noise of the digital sensor. The right shot was made with ISO 80. This low ISO setting produced clean results with no apparent noise levels

Keep in mind that in some lighting conditions, the only real option to take a photograph is to increase the sensitivity. This is not so bad because you can perform noise reduction later in the post-processing step, so it is preferred to get a noisy image than no image at all in bad lighting conditions.

Post-Processing

The final step in producing the photograph is the post-processing done in the computer using digital image processing tools. This is the equivalent of the dark room in film cameras. Using image processing tools, the photographer can bring out the best in their photographs. He can enhance the image, remove unwanted objects, change colors, merge different images, reduce noise, change contrast or brightness, alter the size or orientation of the photograph, crop, and virtually anything that you can think of, which is possible with today's available tools. Professional photographers usually apply several filters and changes to their images before they release them. Please note that although image processing can really improve your photos, you still need to take an interesting image to begin with. Many times, it is much easier to reshoot the subject than trying to fix the image later in the computer. For example, if you want to add a motion effect to an object, use a slow shutter speed; blurring it later will not look as good.

This book is based on this third step of the process of taking a photograph, digital image processing. Different techniques needed for image processing are explained, from the simplest geometric transforms such as resizing, to the more complex techniques such as HDR, or creating panoramas. The main difference between this book and any other image processing book for photography is that it is completely based on free software; therefore, you can use the tools described here for processing your images without paying anything and obtaining great-looking photographs.

The software product you'll be using most in this book is Gimp, which is a very powerful image manipulation program. It has many options that allow you to process your images in many different ways. It is one of the most versatile programs out there.

UFRaw is a nice program that allows you to develop RAW files and also works as a plug-in for Gimp.

Another software product that I selected is Qtpfsgui, which allows you to create HDR images from ordinary images. The nice thing about it is that it is simpler to use than it is to pronounce its name.

Hugin is used for creating panoramic images. This software lets you load normal images and after a few clicks, you will have a stunning panorama.

Imagemagick is another software product that I will be using. It may be seen as a little more advanced than some, but it really makes things easy when you want to work with thousands of images. The main difference of this program is that it uses the command line, which can be better or worse, depending on the user and the context.

Exiftool is another command-line utility. I wanted to include this software because it really is the best of its class. It allows you to read and write all the metadata (data about data) of your images and do many other things. You can even read stuff like the temperature of the camera when a particular photo was taken.

Summary

Now that you have a solid understanding of how a photograph is created and how the controls and components of your camera affect your photographs, we can explore the specific aspects of digital images.

CHAPTER 2

■ ■ ■

Digital Images

After reading the previous chapter, you are now able to control your camera so that you can capture the exact type of photograph that you want. When you are out in the field taking photographs, you can already apply the concepts that you have learned so far.

In this chapter, I will show you everything that you need to know about digital images. Understanding what a digital image is will help you to get better results while you are working in your digital darkroom.

Vector Images vs. Raster Images

A digital image is a set of bits (zeroes and ones) that represents an image. That set of bits is created following a specific digital image format so that different programs can understand it. There are two main categories of digital images; one of them is called *vector images* and the other, *raster images*.

Vector images are formed using mathematical equations such as lines, points, polygons, and others. Since every object in the image is defined using an equation, making changes to the image is relatively easy; only the parameters of the equation are changed. If you want to resize, change the color, or move the objects, you can just change their properties to the new values. This type of format is commonly used for graphic designers to create images with a level of detail not as rich as a photograph but with the ability to maintain their quality at different sizes, such as logos, icons, fonts, diagrams, and so forth. If you are interested in editing vector images, I recommend that you use Inkscape, which is excellent free software for that purpose.

Raster images, on the other hand, are represented using pixels. A *pixel*, also called a picture element, is the smallest measurable unit in raster images. It can be thought of as a colored dot. When all the pixels of the image are looked at together, the image is perceived. Making changes to this type of image is done by changing the color of the pixels or changing the number of pixels that represent the image. You can see this difference in Figure 2-1. Raster images are commonly used in photography where high detail is needed. From now on, this book will be based only on this category of images.

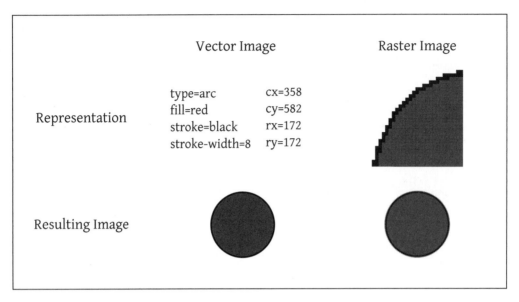

Figure 2-1. *This diagram shows the differences in the representation of a circle with a black border as a vector and a raster image. Vector images are created using mathematical formulas. Raster images on the other hand are formed using many small colored dots called pixels.*

Resolution

The *resolution* of an image is the number of pixels that are used to represent the image. For example, if the resolution of an image is 2,816 × 2,112, it means that the image has a width of 2,816 pixels and a height of 2,112 pixels. You can also say that the resolution of that image is 6 megapixels (MP) because 2,816 × 2,112 is 5,947,392, which is roughly 6 million pixels, or 6MP.

In general, the more pixels used to represent an image, the better it will look. This is true up to a limit where no gain in quality is perceived by the human eye. This limit depends on the use of the image. Today, there are two main uses for digital photographs: displaying them on a computer screen (or a similar device) and printing them on paper (or a similar surface).

Resolution for Computer Displays

For regular computer screen display (e-mail, web pages, online photo albums, and so forth), you usually do not need a very large resolution. In most cases, you would need a much smaller image than most cameras can deliver. Take, for example, the High Definition standard (Full-HD). It consists of 1920 × 1080 pixels, which translates into little more than 2MP. This means that you only need a 2MP image to make the photograph look good because it is more than enough to cover most of today's computer display resolutions. Please note that in the future, larger screen resolutions may become available, increasing this number. Any larger resolution will be resized to fit the screen (or you will need to use scroll bars to see it completely). Note that this is true only if you want to look at the picture as a whole; if you want to inspect details by zooming in on certain places of the image, you would need a larger resolution (as large as the level of details you want to inspect).

For comparing how the image resolution impacts the photograph visual quality, I will show you how different resolutions look when the photograph is displayed at a fixed size on the screen. Figures 2-2 through 2-4 were scaled to the same viewing size of 704 × 528 without interpolation. This size is similar but slightly larger than the common normal sizes shown in popular online photo albums. Note how the quality improves when the resolution is increased.

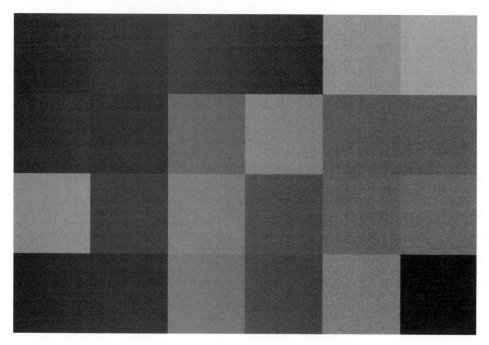

Figure 2-2. This image shows a photograph with a tiny resolution of 6 × 4 pixels. The resolution is so low that you can actually count the pixels in the image. At this resolution, the image looks so bad that the contents of the photo cannot be distinguished.

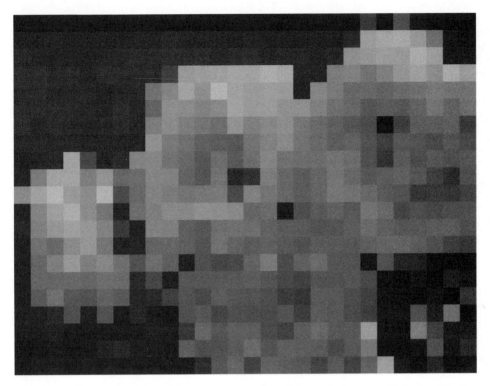

Figure 2-3. *Here, a resolution of 28 × 21 was used. At this resolution, very little detail is shown; you can only tell that there is some kind of light object on a darker background.*

Figure 2-4. *At 704 × 528 pixels, the image looks very good. All the edges are smooth and no pixel is noticeable. This was the size of the image opened in a regular photo viewer on my computer.*

Resolution for Printing

For printing, usually a high-resolution photograph is needed. The recommended number of pixels used to print a photograph depends on the size of the print. Larger prints require larger resolutions. For good-quality prints, you need at least 300 pixels per inch (ppi). For example, if you want to print a 6MP image, it would print well at around 9 × 7 inches, although it is not a common print size and would need to be cropped, as explained later. For acceptable quality, you would need at least 200 ppi. Less than that would print a poorly defined photo. In the case of large billboards, you usually can't get enough resolution for printing them with high quality, but because they are usually seen from far away, you can get away with it with a lower-resolution image. Table 2-1 lists some common print sizes and their required resolutions.

Table 2-1. This table shows the minimum recommended image resolution when printing at different sizes and qualities.

Common print sizes	Good quality	Acceptable quality
6 × 4 inches (15 × 10 cms)	2.2MP	1.0MP
7 × 5 inches (18 × 12 cms)	3.2MP	1.4MP
10 × 8 inches (25 × 20 cms)	7.2MP	3.2MP

The *print size* or *print resolution* is how large or small the digital image will appear on paper. By default, most digital cameras set this number to 72 ppi, although this does not affect the pixels of the image at all. This number is only for telling the printer how large or small you want to print your photograph. You can change this number easily in most modern image processing software without changing the image resolution, as explained later in the book.

Aspect Ratio

A digital camera's sensors are nowadays measured in MP. This represents the total number of pixels of the resulting image (width x height) but gives no information about its aspect ratio (width to height). In general, point-and-shoot digital cameras have an aspect ratio of 4:3, which is the standard definition in television and monitors (as opposed to high-definition, which has an aspect ratio of 16:9). On the other hand, digital single lens reflex cameras (DSLRs) usually have an aspect ratio of 3:2, which is the same as the 35mm film format. You can easily check the aspect ratio of your camera just by looking at the size of any image that you have taken with it and calculate the width-to-height ratio (take its width and divide it by its height). For example, if the result is 1.3333…, you know that the image has a 4:3 aspect ratio. On the other hand, if the result is 1.5, then you know that your camera produces images with a 3:2 aspect ratio.

Aspect ratio is particularly important when printing a digital image. There are different standard sizes in print and in digital images, so part of your image may need to be taken away to fit the print standard. Figure 2-5 shows some of the more common print sizes. You can read the next chapter to learn how to crop your images to fit nicely into the desired print size or you can just let the photo developer arbitrarily cut your picture.

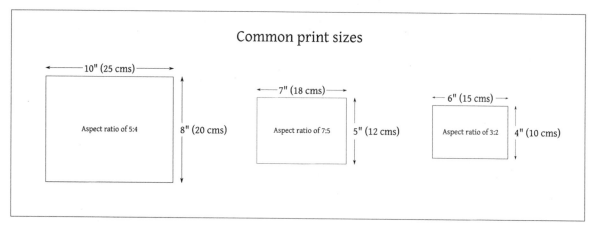

Figure 2-5. Some of the most common print sizes in photography. Note how the aspect ratio is not the same in these three sizes.

Figure 2-6 shows an example of a photograph that was taken at an aspect ratio of 4:3. If you wanted to print it at 6 × 4 inches (aspect ratio of 3:2), you'd need to crop it before sending it to the printer so you know how the image will look like in print and make any changes if necessary.

Figure 2-6. The highlighted areas show the regions that are commonly cropped to change the aspect ratio from 4:3 to 3:2. A similar effect appears when a widescreen film is seen on a standard TV; black bars above and below the images are added so that it can fit without changing its aspect ratio. This effect is known as letterboxing.

Color

The contents of a digital image are *pixels*, or colored dots. To understand what color is, first we need to think about light. Light is one type of electromagnetic radiation. Other types of electromagnetic radiation are AM and FM radio, Wi-Fi, Bluetooth, microwaves, infrared, and x-rays. Although it may sound strange at first, all of these are the same kind of thing; electromagnetic radiation. The only difference between them is their wavelength. Humans are able to see electromagnetic radiation that has a wavelength of roughly 400 to 700 nanometers (nm) as colors. Other animals are able to sense different parts of the electromagnetic spectrum and therefore are able to see different colors that humans cannot see. Other wavelengths are sensed by humans but in different ways; for example, infrared light is sensed as heat.

The experience of color in nature is a process that combines the eye and the brain. The eyes act as light receptors and the brain interprets the data from the eyes as visual information. Color is the wavelength of the incoming electromagnetic radiation. As you can see in the diagram, the wavelength of the electromagnetic radiation has a full spectrum of continuous values, which means that there is an infinite number of possible colors in nature.

Color is very important to digital images. In a digital environment, a specific number of bits are used to represent information. This means that we cannot store an infinite number of colors. We need to allocate a certain number of bits to be used to represent color. This number is called *color depth* and for understanding what those numbers represent, you need to learn about *color spaces*. Those are the two subjects that I will show you now.

Color Depth

Color depth is the number of bits that are used to represent the color of each pixel in a digital image. The more bits used, the more unique colors can be used in the image. When more unique colors are used, the image looks more natural to the human eye up to a limit where no difference is noted when increasing the color depth.

If you use a color depth of only 1 bit, the resulting image will only have 2 possible colors. These two colors can actually be any of the available colors that the computer can reproduce, but usually black and white are used in this scenario. If you increase the color depth to 8 bits, you are able to use up to 256 (2^8) different colors, which is normally used for representing a grayscale image or a reduced set of colors. Using 24 bits gives you more than 16 million unique colors. When increasing the color depth to more than 24 bits, most humans cannot tell the difference from the original with 24 bits; that is why this color depth is often called *truecolor*.

You can think of color depth as a third component of the quality of an image, with the first two being width and height (see Figure 2-7).

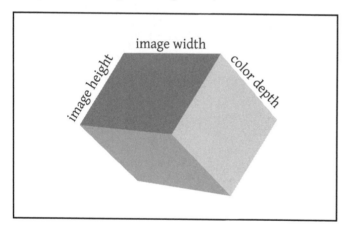

Figure 2-7. Three concepts that are related to image quality. Think of image quality as the volume of this box; the larger the image width, height, and color depth are, the better image quality is achieved, up to a limit where no difference is noted by the human eye.

For obtaining optimal results in your images, it is recommended to use a depth of color of at least 24 bits when working with color photography and 8 bits when working with black and white photography (which really means grayscale).

Color Spaces

Humans have trichromatic vision, which in simple terms means that the human vision is based on three receptors: one for red, another for green, and another for blue. In the same way, for representing a color, there are many different *color spaces*, or models, which usually have three or four channels.

RGB

One of the most commonly used color spaces is RGB. In this space, there are three channels: red, green, and blue. Every color in this space is created using a combination of these three channels. The combination of colors is made based on additive color mixing, which is how light works. Starting with a black surface, light is projected onto it, obtaining different colors. For example, if you have red and green lights and you project them with the same intensity or brightness onto the same black surface, the reflected light will appear as yellow.

In the case of a digital image in the RGB color space, each pixel is defined as (r, g, b) where r, g, and b are the values of each channel. The possible values for each channel go from 0 (no light with that color) to the number of possible values for that channel minus one. For example, if the color depth is 24 bits, then each of the three channels has 8 bits of depth, therefore every channel has values that range from 0 to 255. In that scenario, a pure red color is represented by (255, 0, 0) because it needs the maximum intensity in the red channel, and no light from the green or blue channels. In the same way, a pure yellow is represented by (255, 255, 0) because red and green added together result in yellow. All the colors and different shades are obtained using different combinations of these three values, as shown in Figure 2-8.

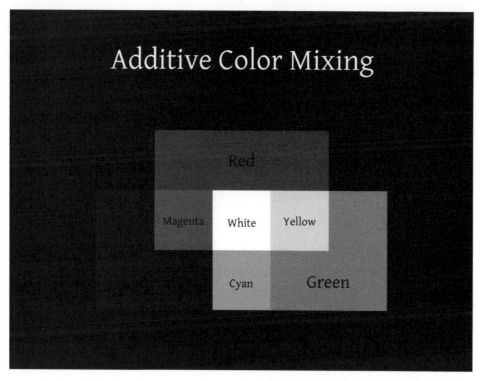

Figure 2-8. *This figure shows how additive color mixing works. When light of different colors is projected onto a black surface, it is mixed, producing new colors. The mix of all visible light is white. Note that the primary colors in the RGB color space are the secondary colors in the cyan, magenta, yellow, and black (CMYK) color space, and vice versa.*

This color space is widely used in such hardware as printers, displays, and digital cameras, as you can see in Figure 2-9. Although an RGB color space is device-dependant, most of the current devices use the same RGB color space, sRGB, which is a standard RGB color space created by Microsoft and HP. This standardization eases color management, which is the mapping of color between input and output devices.

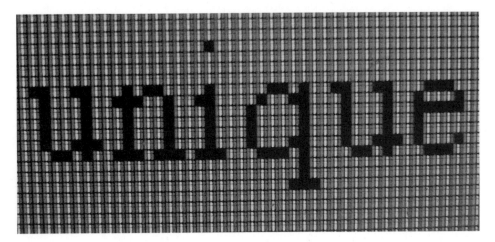

Figure 2-9. *A close up of an LCD screen showing black text over a white background. The colors are formed using additive color mixing; black is made without any light and white is made using the maximum intensity for red, green, and blue for each pixel.*

CMYK

This color space is commonly used for printing. It is based on four channels: cyan, magenta, yellow, and black. The colors in this space are formed using subtractive color mixing, which is how such pigments as ink work. Starting from a white paper, colored inks subtract light from the paper (less light is reflected), obtaining a different color. Only three channels are needed to represent all the colors (cyan, magenta, and yellow), but for practical reasons, black was also added to the color space. By changing the values of each channel, all the different colors of this space are produced, as shown in Figure 2-10.

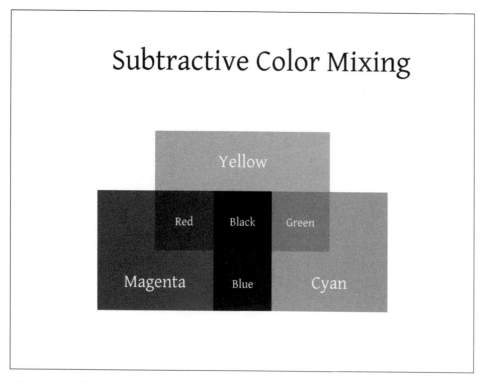

Figure 2-10. This figure shows how subtractive color mixing works. When pigments of different colors (such as ink) are put onto a white surface, less light is reflected from the surface, producing new colors. The mix of all colored pigments is black (the surface does not reflect any visible light). Note that the primary colors in the CMYK color space are the secondary colors in the RGB color space, and vice versa.

HSV

HSV stands for hue, saturation, and value. In this color space, the hue represents the primary color, and the saturation and value represent the specific shade for that hue. The main use of this color space is for creating better interaction with humans because of our usual tendency to recognize different colors (hue) at different shades (saturation and value). It is more natural for humans to first select a solid color and then select a specific shade for it, such as light blue or dark red, for example, than selecting a specific value from RGB.

YUV

YUV color space is composed of the luma (Y) channel, which is the image brightness, and two chrominance channels (U and V) that describe the specific color of the image. It has been mainly used for encoding analog video and television.

Lab

Lab is one of the most complex and complete color spaces available. Its creation was inspired by how humans perceive color. There are three channels where L represents lightness, a represents how red/green the color is, and b represents how yellow/blue the color is. The a and b channels were created based on how human color perception works.

File Formats

There are different formats for storing the pixels of a digital image. Because we are going to modify the contents of digital images, it is very important to know which file format to use, since some formats are lossy while some are lossless.

Lossy formats compress the original image, removing certain details of it so that it still looks similar to the human eye but with a smaller file size. This means that some data is lost in the process. The nice thing about them is that the file sizes can get really small. The bad thing is that, in some cases, the image loses too much information and it does not look as good as the original. Also, every time you save in a lossy format, the process is repeated, degrading your image even more.

Lossless formats, on the other hand, encode the original image in a way so that it doesn't lose any details of the original image. They can still compress images, but not as much as the lossy formats. The nice thing about these formats is that they always preserve the full quality of your original image. The bad thing is that they may take more space in your disk than the lossy ones.

These are the most common raster image file formats.

JPG

JPG, or JPEG (for Joint Photographic Experts Group), is the most common file format in digital photography. It supports a color depth of 24 bits (3 color channels of 8 bits each). Almost every digital camera is able to write images using this format and it is widely supported in different viewing programs. It produces small file sizes using *lossy compression*. Every time you save an image in this format, the quality degrades because a lossy compression is made. Lossy compression removes details of the image so that it can be represented with less information. It uses complex mathematical analysis to remove the least noticeable bits of information of the image so that the human eye can't tell the difference. Note that you can view a JPG image as many times as you want without altering its quality; the quality degrades only when it is saved. Also, the loss in quality in most of the cases is very small and almost unnoticeable by the human eye if saved in a high-quality setting. However, saving a JPG file several times may lead to a considerable loss in image quality. It is therefore recommended that digital images are saved in a lossless format while post processing them, and only saving to JPG as the last step when no further modifications are going to be done.

This format also supports a feature called *progressive JPEG*. This feature allows you to save the image intelligently so that the information is ordered in a specific way so that different resolutions of the image are being presented to the user until the complete image is received. This is useful for large images being transferred to computers via a slow connection.

GIF

GIF stands for Graphics Interchange Format. It can store a depth of color of only 8 bits (256 colors). It handles transparency in a very basic form (each pixel is either transparent or not). The main advantage of this file format is that it can be used to save animations. Also, because it is an old format, it is very compatible with old versions of web browsers and other software. It uses lossless compression. This format has been used mostly for displaying graphics and animations on web pages. Because of the limitation on the number of colors, it is not recommended to use this format for storing digital photographs.

PNG

PNG stands for Portable Network Graphics. It is a publicly available and useable version of the GIF format. It can handle a color depth of up to 48 bits (3 color channels of 16 bits each). It has much better support for transparency than GIF; it allows you to have different levels of transparency for each pixel (alpha channel). The support for this format started to grow since its origin in 1995, and today it is widely supported. Overall, PNG is a better format than GIF; it offers a better compression, it can store more colors, it has a better transparency support, and so forth. The only disadvantage of PNG over GIF is that it cannot save animations. Because of its great color depth, browser compatibility, and its lossless compression, it is a recommended format for digital photography. Compared to JPG, PNG gives you better image quality at the expense of larger files sizes mainly due to the lossless format used.

TIFF

TIFF stands for Tagged Image File Format. It is one of the most flexible image formats. It allows saving more than just one image per file, which explains why it is the standard format for document imaging. Also, it can store advanced data types such as floating points, mostly used in scientific imaging. Also, it supports data stored in different color spaces, such as CMYK or RGB. This image format gives the option of compressing the image using lossless or lossy algorithms (or no compression at all). This image format also can contain vector image information in conjunction with the raster image information. It supports a color depth of up to 48 bits (16 bits per channel) and also supports transparency. Because all of its options, it is suitable for professional digital photography, especially for archiving and printing.

OpenEXR

This format is an open standard for describing high dynamic range images (HDR). The file extension that it uses is EXR. You can use it with lossy or lossless compression. It was created and actively used by Industrial Light & Magic on motion pictures. There is a publicly available library for reading and writing images in this format.

Which Format Should You Use?

You should use the TIFF format for serious professional photography that needs the maximum possible quality and flexibility at the expense of bad support for web usage and large file sizes. This format is excellent for storing high-quality images.

For everyday usage, the JPG format is the winner, having the smallest image file size, but at the expense of decreasing its quality every time it is saved and the reduced color depth.

PNG stands in between, offering lossless compression, high color depth, and being well supported for web page usage.

Only use GIF for web animations and not for digital photography because of its poor color depth.

OpenEXR is great for storing HDR images. Because there is a publicly available library, it is already compatible with many programs.

Note that these are general image file formats. There are many other file formats that are specific to image processing programs. While you are working with those programs, it is recommended that you always save your images in the program's own format. By doing this, you will preserve all the information you need to continue your work, such as layers, for example. Once you finish your post-processing, you can then decide to save the final image into one of the previously described formats for normal viewing.

Starting to Use the Tools

I would like to use this opportunity to get you started with using some of the tools that I'll show you in this book.

First, I will show you how to change between file formats using Gimp and Imagemagick. Gimp is a graphical tool that allows you to make many changes to your images and is very easy to use. Imagemagick is a command-line utility that lets you do similar things as Gimp.

Changing File Formats with Gimp

Gimp may be already installed in your computer. If it is not, please go to the appendix where you can read the instructions for how to install it.

You can always change the format of your images using Gimp; just load the image and select Save As from the File menu. The dialog shown in Figure 2-11 will appear.

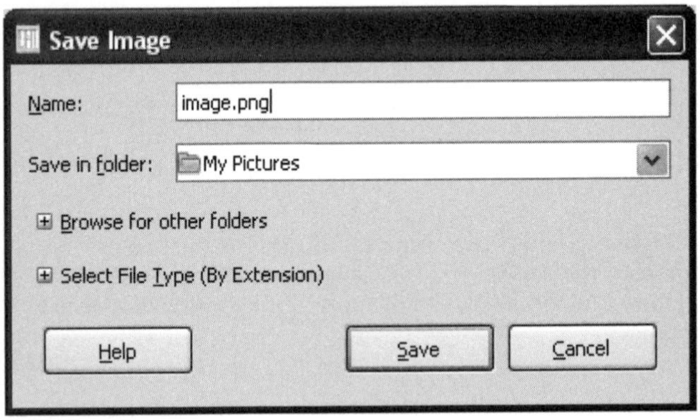

Figure 2-11. Saving an image in a different format in Gimp

You can just type in any extension that you want for your image and then click Save or if you prefer, you can click on Select File Type for a comprehensive list of supported formats.

This is acceptable if you only want to change the format of a couple of images, but if you want to change a lot of images, it is better to use ImageMagick.

Changing File Formats with ImageMagick

If you haven't already done so, install ImageMagick in your computer. You can read how to do so in the appendix.

After you download and install ImageMagick, just go to the command line and type the following:

```
mogrify -format [outputFormat] *.[inputFormat]
```

For example, if you want to create a PNG version of all your JPG files, go to the folder where your images are stored using the command line and then just type:

```
mogrify -format png *.jpg
```

Summary

In this chapter, you learned everything you need to know related to digital images. You know how resolution and color depth can affect the image quality and why the aspect ratio is especially important when printing an image. Also, I showed you the differences between common color spaces. You also learned about file formats and which one you should use.

Now that you have a solid background on digital images, it is finally time to start learning how to process your photos. Let's start with some of the most common and simplest ways of processing your images: resizing, cropping, and more.

CHAPTER 3

■ ■ ■

Geometric Transforms

In the previous chapters, you gained a solid background on photography and digital images. Now is the time for you to start learning how to process your images, and I will start with some of the most common and simple tasks that every photographer has to do: resizing, cropping, rotating, and flipping images. These operations are known as *geometric transforms* and they are the focus of this chapter. Note that the term *transform* simply refers to any qualitative change produced in an image. For showing you how to perform these operations, I will use Gimp and ImageMagick, which you already know from the previous chapter.

Geometric transforms are changes to the image that produce a different representation of the original image or part of it, most of the time using more or fewer pixels than the original. Some of these transforms may alter significantly the quality of the original image; others reduce its resolution; and only a few of them maintain the same pixels of the original. Because of this, I recommend that you use them only once instead of multiple times. For example, if you want to rotate an image by 60 degrees, start with the original and rotate it 60 degrees, do not rotate it 20 degrees first and then 40 degrees, because the image quality will degrade each time. The same holds true for resizing; if you don't like the new size, go back and resize again from the original.

Resizing an image or rotating it in any angle different than a multiple of 90° will reduce the quality of the original image; although depending on how it is done, the quality loss can be almost imperceptible to the human eye.

Cropping an image will effectively reduce its resolution but will maintain the quality of the cropped section. Poor resolution is most noticeable when printing a small crop from a larger original picture. Although, if done correctly, it can improve how an image looks because of changes in the final composition.

Flipping an image or rotating it in multiples of 90° are the only few exceptions where a geometric transform preserves the quality of the original image. This is because no pixel value is changed; they are only moved to another position.

Note that there are also other geometric transforms offered in Gimp that I will not include in this chapter, such as Move, Shear, or Perspective. Move allows you to simply move a region of the image around and Shear is a subset of Perspective, which I am going to cover later in the book for correcting perspective distortion.

Resizing

Resizing is one of the most common changes made to a digital image. As the resolution of the digital cameras' sensors gets larger, so do the images they produce. This is a good thing if you are planning to print your images or look at fine details, but if you want to display them on a web page, in a presentation, or even send them through an e-mail, you should diminish the size of the image to decrease the file size and to make them fit easily on the screen. For other applications, you may as well want to augment the size of the image or even change its *aspect ratio*, which is obtained by increasing or decreasing the size of one side of the image more than the top or bottom, or vice-versa.

In the case where the resulting image is smaller than the original, the idea is to try to represent the original image using fewer pixels. On the other hand, when the resulting image is larger than the original, the objective is to create extra pixels so that the size of the image is larger but the scene shown in the image itself is as visually as close as possible to the original. You can represent the original image with more or fewer pixels in many different ways and each of them can produce different results that can greatly affect the quality of the final image.

Resizing Methods

One of the simplest methods for resizing an image is by using a technique called *Nearest Neighbor*. This technique only uses the values from the original image to generate the resized version of it.

When increasing the size of an image, every pixel is copied as many times as needed to fill the new image. When decreasing the size of an image, only pixels that are selected at regular intervals are used to fill the smaller image. The Nearest Neighbor technique has the problem of generating images that appear blocky or pixelized, similar to the problem of not having enough resolution in the image. Figure 3-1 shows how this looks.

Another approach is to use *Linear Interpolation*. This method generates new pixel values (or colors) based on the surrounding pixels. Normally, a simple average of those values is used to generate the new pixels. This method produces better results than the Nearest Neighbor technique, but the final image is generally very blurred (without well-defined borders).

Although the previous methods may be easy to implement, some of the most effective methods are more mathematically complex. There are many of them, some use more complex interpolations and others are based on advanced mathematical concepts. One example is the *Windowed Sinc* filters that use the *Sinc* function, which is mathematically proven to be a good method for resizing. Another example is the *Cubic* family of filters, which was created by image experts in an attempt to obtain fast and accurate methods for resizing. The results are shown in Figure 3-1.

In general, *Windowed Sinc* filters (like *Lanczos*) are the best choice for resizing photographs, particularly when scaling down the images (making them smaller). *Cubic* filters are also a good choice. Those are especially good for scaling up images (making them larger). Stay away from simpler methods, as they do not produce good quality images.

Figure 3-1. *The left image shows an enlargment of 20 × using the Nearest Neighbor method. Note the poor quality of the edges where blocks of pixels are visible. On the right side, the same image was resized using the Cubic method producing a much better image.*

Resizing with Gimp

Gimp offers a simple selection of resizing algorithms. If you need to resize a couple of photographs, this is the easiest way to do it. Open your image and select Image → Scale Image.

In the *Scale Image* dialog box (see Figure 3-2), you can define the new size of the image in pixels, percentage, or any other metrics shown in the menu. The method that Gimp will use for the resize is the one that you select under Interpolation.

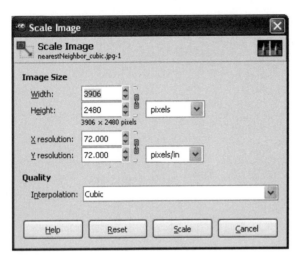

Figure 3-2. The different options for resizing an image in GIMP

Gimp offers the following resizing methods: None, Linear, Cubic, Sinc (Lanczos). None is the one described as Nearest Neighbor, and the rest are self explanatory. As explained before, for shrinking photographs in general, it is recommended to use the Sinc method and for enlarging photos, the Cubic method. Note that this is not a strict rule and you can experiment with both to see which one gives you better results for any particular photograph.

It is important to note that there is also an option for resizing the *Canvas*, which is a different thing. You can access that option in Gimp by going into Image → Canvas Size. The Canvas basically is the image container. Most of the time, you will want the Canvas to be the same size of your image, although if you want to make a collage for example, you will need to resize your Canvas first to the size of the collage and then start adding the other photos. As you can see in Figure 3-3, I decided to leave space for putting two images side by side. Because I wanted to change the aspect ratio of the Canvas, I had to click on the chain icon so that it allows me to change its width and height independently.

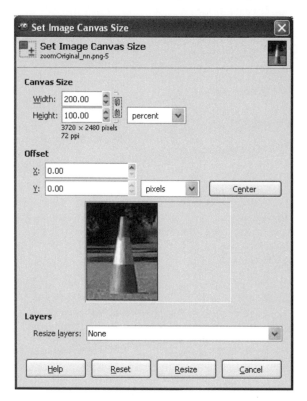

Figure 3-3. The different options for resizing the Canvas in GIMP

Resizing with ImageMagick

When resizing more than a couple of pictures, ImageMagick provides an excellent solution. Because it is a command-line program, you can resize many pictures with just one command instead of having to open all of them as separate windows in Gimp.

ImageMagick also offers many advanced options for resizing. For example, it supports several *Windowed Sinc* and *Cubic* filters, as well as other methods not mentioned here. Also, it supports many optional configurations for every method to achieve maximum control over the resize.

By default, ImageMagick chooses the best filter depending on the type of image and if you are shrinking or enlarging the photograph. For this book, we will only be using the default options, as they are almost always the ones that produce the best results. Keep in mind that ImageMagick provides many more options than those described here, where I've limited the options for simplicity.

The following code resizes Image.jpg into ImageResized.jpg:

```
convert Image.jpg -resize 1024x768 ImageResized.jpg
```

ImageMagick is always trying to make the final image look the best. When resizing, it will try to preserve the aspect ratio of the original image. Therefore, in the previous example, the final image may not have a resolution of exactly 102×768, but actually less. This is because ImageMagick tries to fit the original image into the resolution the user gave. Normally, this produces a good-looking image.

If you want to resize the image to exactly the dimensions you enter, you can add one character, the exclamation mark, and ImageMagick will just do that:

```
convert Image.jpg -resize 1024x768! ImageResized.jpg
```

In the previous example, `Image.jpg` was resized to `ImageResized.jpg`, which has exactly 1024×768 pixels.

For resizing a group of pictures, all you need to do is the following command:

```
convert *.jpg -resize 1024x768 ImageResized.jpg
```

The previous command will generate a list of images named `ImageResized-0.jpg`, `ImageResized-1.jpg`, `ImageResized-2.jpg`, and so on, based on the number of pictures that exist in that directory. Keep in mind that you can change the filenames and file types to anything you need in particular.

Resizing Print Size

When you are printing an image, you need to specify to the printer the size of the print that you want. You don't need to alter the image's original resolution; you just need to change the image print size, which is different than the image size. It is measured in length units such as inches or millimeters, and it is the size of the printed photograph that will come out of the printer.

Changing the Print Size with Gimp

One of the easiest ways to change the image print size for a couple of photographs is by using Gimp. Just open the picture with Gimp and select Image → Print Size. The dialog shown in Figure 3-4 appears.

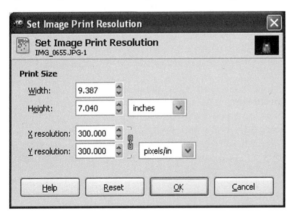

Figure 3-4. Setting the image print size or resolution using Gimp

You can either change the exact size of the print or give a specific resolution and Gimp will calculate the other value for you. For this figure, I used a 6MP image; note that by selecting a resolution of 300 ppi (good quality), Gimp automatically changes the print size to about 9×7 inches, which is the same size that I suggested for a 6MP image in the previous chapter.

Changing the Print Size with ImageMagick

If you want to change the print size for a large number of photos, it may be a little uncomfortable to open all of them with Gimp and change each value independently. For this task, it is usually better to use the command-line program ImageMagick.

Let's first change the print resolution to 300×300 for all the JPG files in the current directory using ImageMagick. The syntax for doing this is the following:

```
mogrify -density [XResolutionxYResolution] [ImagePath]
```

For example, if you want to change the print resolution of the file IMG_0630.JPG to 300×300 ppi, you can achieve that by doing this:

```
mogrify -density 300x300 IMG_0630.JPG
```

The default unit is ppi. If you want to use another unit, you can call the command that is presented next. Some example values for the units are PixelsPerInch and PixelsPerCentimeter.

```
mogrify -density [XResolutionxYResolution] -units [NameOfUnits] [ImagePath]
```

Now that we know how to change the value for one image, it is easy to modify the code to change any number of pictures. The simplest way of doing this is to move all the images you want to change in a specific folder and then run the following code:

```
mogrify *.JPG -density 300x300
```

This code assumes that your pictures have a JPG file extension, which is the most common. Change it accordingly to any specific image file format your images are in. Also, note that in Linux, the file names are case-sensitive, so for instance, JPG is different than jpg. You can see the current print resolution of an image with this code:

```
identify -format "%x x %y" [filename]
```

With this code, you would be able to see the print resolution of the example image:

```
identify -format "%x x %y" IMG_0630.JPG
```

Cropping

Cropping trims the image to a specific region. When you crop an image, the quality of the output region remains the same as the original region (which is not true when resizing). Cropping is often useful for correcting composition problems. Also, you can use it to completely remove unwanted objects from the scene or adjust the composition to more reflect the rule of thirds, or to change the image to a different aspect ratio.

The implementation of a crop operation is very simple. You only keep the pixels that you selected; the rest are deleted. This means that this is a completely different approach than resizing an image. The nice thing about cropping is that the image will maintain the original quality. Figure 3-6 shows a crop of the image in Figure 3-5. I changed the aspect ratio of the image just by cropping out some areas at the top and the bottom.

Figure 3-5. *This is the original image. It is being cropped to change the aspect ratio to make a different composition.*

Figure 3-6. *This is the cropped version of the image. Note how the aspect ratio changed while maintaining the original image quality.*

You can also use crop to remove distractions and bring focus on the area you wish the viewer to notice, as Figures 3-7 and 3-8 demonstrate.

Figure 3-7. *This is the original image. The intention was to shoot the sign on the tree, but there turned out to be many distractions in the image.*

Figure 3-8. *This is a cropped and resized version of the previous image. You can see the sign with more details and without distractions.*

Cropping with Gimp

To crop images in Gimp, open your image and select Tools → Transform Tools → Crop. Alternatively, you can press Shift+C. Also, you can click on the Crop tool icon in the Toolbox, as shown in Figure 3-9.

Figure 3-9. The Crop tool selected in the Toolbox in Gimp

Now you can select the region you want to crop by clicking and dragging the mouse. It is not necessary to do it precisely because you can change the region afterwards. You will see something similar to Figure 3-10.

Figure 3-10. This image shows the region that is going to be cropped in Gimp.

Something nice about cropping with Gimp is that you can add guides. These guides provide you with extra information that can help you make better compositions. Remember the composition rules from Chapter 1? Well, here is your chance to apply that knowledge. You can select different guides, such as the rule of thirds, so that you can move it around until the points of interest are aligned with the guide. After the guide is aligned with the points or lines of interest, such as the horizon, you can proceed to crop.

For enabling these guides, you have to select one from the drop-down menu. This menu is located in the Toolbox window under the crop tab, as seen in Figure 3-11.

Figure 3-11. This image shows how to enable different guides for better composition. The rule of thirds guide is selected for this example.

You can resize the region, moving the cursor to one of the edges of it and dragging it to the desired location. Dragging the corners allow you to resize the region in both directions at the same time. Also, you can move the region by dragging it with the mouse. To crop the image, just press the Enter key on your keyboard. Figure 3-12 shows the results. You can always go back to the original image by pressing Control+Z or selecting Edit → Undo.

Figure 3-12. This figure shows the result of cropping an image after pressing the Enter key.

Cropping with ImageMagick

You can also crop images using ImageMagick. This may be useful in some specific cases, but in general I would suggest using Gimp for this particular task because of the benefits of a graphical interface and the guides that it offers. Well, let's face, it is really hard to crop an image that you can't see. There are, however, some general cases where you may want to automatically crop your image, such as removing letterboxing from an image sequence. The command needed for cropping using ImageMagick has the following syntax:

```
convert *.jpg -crop [width]x[height]+[posX]+[posY] croppedImage.jpg
```

The arguments *width* and *height* represent the size of the cropped region. The *posX* and *posY* values represent the offset from the top left corner of the image. You can change the *posX* and *posY* values accordingly to crop regions located at different positions. For example, if you want to generate a 200 × 300 crop from the top left of the images, you should type this command:

```
convert *.jpg -crop 200x300+0+0 croppedImage.jpg
```

Rotating

Rotating the image is generally used for straightening photographs. Rotating an image in any angle different than a multiple of 90° alters the contents of image, degrading its quality, so it is recommended not to use it many times. If you rotate an image and do not achieve the results you expected, it is better to undo the changes and start again from the original than continuing iteratively rotating the image.

Like resizing, rotating changes the contents of the image. This means that we also have to choose a method for recomputing the pixels, as we did when resizing. Similar to the resize, selecting a Cubic or Sinc method would produce the best results.

Rotating with Gimp

Gimp is useful for rotating images. Open your image and select Tools → Transform Tools → Rotate.

As you can see in Figure 3-13, rotating an image is achieved by simply changing the angle in the Rotate dialog box or by dragging the mouse over the image. Also, you can select the center of the rotation. For straightening photographs, this position should be set to the center of the image (which is the default), but feel free to try other values to create different effects.

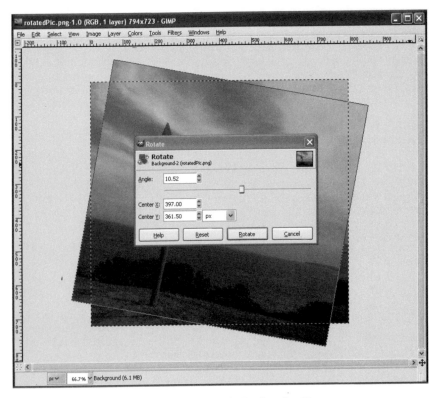

Figure 3-13. This image shows the Rotate dialog box for Gimp.

After you select the Rotate tool, the Toolbox window, shown in Figure 3-14, shows the available options for the rotation. Similarly to the guides when cropping, here we can add guides for straightening horizons or vertical lines. You can enable this guide by selecting Grid in the Preview option. With the help of this guide, you can align the photo with vertical/horizontal elements of it such as trees, buildings, and so forth.

As the rotated image will not fit in the original canvas, it is convenient to crop the resulting image to a more useful one. You can do this by selecting Crop to result from the Clipping drop-down menu. You can also increase or decrease the number of grid lines in the Toolbox window to better fit your image. The idea is to change the number of lines so that some of the lines are close to vertical or horizontal elements in your image. Having grid lines close to those elements helps you in the process of selecting a proper position of the grid. For straightening photographs, make sure that Corrective (Backward) is selected under Direction because you want to rotate the image back a certain amount of degrees, not rotating further away. You may wonder why the default is the opposite direction. Well, since Gimp is a general image processing program, it makes sense that a rotation tool will actually rotate an image in the desired direction. In this particular case, we are using this tool as a correction of a rotation already present in the image. This is why you had to choose Corrective instead of the Normal mode.

As you can see, there is also a 15 degrees check box. If you check that, the angles that you can rotate will be constrained into multiples of 15 degrees, which may be simpler for some users. Note that you can get the same results if you hold the Control key while rotating the image.

Figure 3-14. This image shows the rotate options in the toolbox window in the Gimp.

Now we are ready to straighten the image. First, change the angle of the grid using the mouse or the angle slidebar from the Resize dialog box until the guide lines are on top or parallel to the horizontal or vertical lines in your photograph, as shown in Figure 3-15.

Figure 3-15. *Straightening a picture using a grid in Gimp*

Once the grid is correctly placed, the angle value shown in the Rotate dialog box represents the amount of degrees that the image is rotated. Just select *Rotate* and Gimp will produce a straight version of the original, cropped to fit a rectangular region as shown in Figure 3-16.

Figure 3-16. *The result of rotating and cropping the original image*

Note that the canvas is slightly larger than the resulting image. This is the effect of rotating the image. Part of it had to be cropped to make it fit a standard rectangular area. This is easily solved using Gimp. Just select Image → Autocrop Image and you will get an image without the extra canvas, as shown in Figure 3-17.

Figure 3-17. This image shows the final result after rotating and cropping.

Simple rotations are the ones that are multiples of 90°. These do not change the contents of the image—they only change the position—so the quality remains the same. This is normally used for rotating photographs that were taken in a different orientation.

To access this feature in Gimp, you only need to go to Image → Transform. There, you can select any of these three choices: Rotate 90° clockwise, Rotate 90° counter-clockwise, or Rotate 180°. You can see the result of these operations in Figure 3-18.

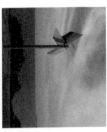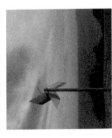

Figure 3-18. The first image on the left shows the original photograph. The next one is how it looks rotated 90° clockwise. The following shows it rotated 90° counter-clockwise. The last picture on the right shows it rotated in 180°.

Rotating with ImageMagick

Some cameras write the orientation in which the photograph was taken in the metadata (remember Chapter 2?). For automatically rotating all images that were taken in a different orientation in a lossless manner, you can use ImageMagick. With the command line, go to the folder where your images are and execute the following code:

```
mogrify -auto-orient *.jpg
```

That way, all the images that were taken with a non-horizontal orientation will be rotated to a horizontal view.

In a more general way, you can also use ImageMagick to rotate all your images by any specific angle with the following command.

```
mogrify -rotate [angle] *.jpg
```

If the angle is positive, it means the rotation is going to be clockwise, and if it is negative, it means counter-clockwise. For example, you can rotate all the images in your current directory by 90 °clockwise with this command:

```
mogrify -rotate 90 *.jpg
```

Remember that only rotations of multiples of 90° are lossless. Any rotation of a different angle will produce an image with less quality than the original.

Flipping

Flipping is a simple transform that inverts the order of the pixels of the image. In this transform, the quality of the original image is maintained the same, although the photograph is reversed. You can flip an image horizontally or vertically. Both operations are lossless because the pixels are only moved around but do not change values.

A vertical flip will produce an upside-down image from the original, similar to, for example, the reflection of trees on a lake. A horizontal flip will produce the same results as looking at the image through a mirror. The results of flipping an image can be seen in Figure 3-19.

Figure 3-19. The first image on the left is the original image. The image in the center is the result of flipping it horizontally. The last image on the right is the result of flipping it vertically.

Flipping with Gimp

To access this feature in Gimp, just open your image, select Image → Transform, and choose between Flip Horizontally and Flip Vertically.

Flipping an image horizontally can give a new look to your image. Sometimes, the flipped version looks better than the original. In those cases, always take care that there aren't any element in the image that may reveal to your viewers that the image was flipped. This can be any type of sign, text, tattoos, clocks, and so forth.

Flipping with ImageMagick

You can always process all your images using ImageMagick. First, open the command line and go to the directory where all the images you want to flip are located. For flipping the images vertically, you need the following code:

```
mogrify -flip *.jpg
```

For flipping the images horizontally, type this code:

```
mogrify -flop *.jpg
```

Summary

After finishing this chapter, you now have a great deal of control over your images. You can now resize them into any resolution that you want, define their print sizes, crop them using guides for obtaining better composition, or change their aspect ratio. Also, you can rotate them, which is very useful for straightening horizons, or even flip them to create a new look.

In the next chapter, you'll be getting into more interesting transforms; you will learn how to make changes in the color of your images.

CHAPTER 4

■ ■ ■

Color Transforms

Color is an illusion. What we normally perceive as color is actually a complex interaction between the eye and the brain.

First, let's think about how we see the world. Light goes to an object, some of it gets absorbed by the object, and the rest bounces back. The bouncing light is how we see that particular object. This means that the color of an object really depends on the light source, the light radiated by nearby objects, and the object, not only on the object by itself.

Now imagine that you are in a room that has only two light sources; one of them is tungsten light, which seems warmer and yellowish, and the other one is a fluorescent light, which seems colder and blueish. If you turn on only the tungsten light and you look at a regular sheet of paper, you would probably say that it looks white. If you turn off the tungsten light and turn on the fluorescent light, you would still probably say that the paper looks white even though the incoming light changed dramatically.

This is explained because humans are extremely good at processing visual information. The brain adjusts the incoming data, trying to make things look the same color under different lighting conditions. This property is called *color constancy* and it means that what we see is sometimes different than what is actually there in real life.

Digital cameras, on the other hand, do not have the same ability. They just store the light that they receive from the real world. And by now we already know that this is different than what we really see. This means that you end up with photos that aren't the same color as what you were looking at when you took the picture.

Most digital images represent color using the RGB color space, which is composed of three channels; one for red, one for green, and one for blue. Putting them together creates the color image. Changing the information of these channels allows us to change how the colors look on the image. Changing the image colors can help to produce an image that looks more similar to what the photographer was looking at when he took the photograph, enhance the overall visual quality of the photograph, or even help in creating artistic effects.

There are many changes that you can apply to a color image, such as brightness, contrast, color saturation, white balance, and so forth. This chapter will explain some of the most important ones.

White Balance

The purpose of *white balance* is to maintain as close as possible the colors of the scene as it was seen by the photographer when he was taking the picture. As discussed earlier, different light sources produce different colors on the objects in the real world. White balance is a technique used to simulate the complex color constancy property that humans have.

White balance only works if you somehow know, or can estimate, the type of lighting that was present when the photograph was taken. Most digital cameras offer white balance presets such as Day Light, Cloudy, Tungsten, Fluorescent, Auto White Balance, and a custom one that allows you to select a white or gray object in the scene and use it as the reference. Auto White Balance is more than enough most of the time, but for some shots you may want to experiment with the other settings that are specially designed to adjust the white balance in those situations.

Color temperature, which is measured in Kelvin degrees, represents the specific spectrum of light, or the specific mixture of colors, that a theoretical black body would emit when heated at the given temperature. This basically means that the specific mixture of colors that different sources of light, such as tungsten bulbs, a candle flame, or day light produce can be expressed using temperature units.

To understand the concept of color temperature, imagine that you hold in your hands a blowtorch that allows you to control the temperature of its flame. If you select a temperature of around 3,000°K, you will see a reddish or yellowish flame, similar to the color of a candle flame or a tungsten light bulb. Now, if you increase the temperature of the flame, you will see how it changes color passing through white at 4,100°K and on up to around 6,500°K or more, where the flame will start looking blueish. That way a specific color temperature, in Kelvin degrees, describes a specific mixture of colors that range from reddish to blueish.

■ **Note** Note that some monitors have a color temperature adjustment. If you want to edit and print your color images professionally, you may need to calibrate your monitor depending on the specific room that you are working in and control the lightning. But that alone can be a topic of an entire book, so we won't go deeper into monitor or printer color calibration.

The white balance is achieved by changing the ratio between the three color channels of the image: red, blue, and green. The most common way to change them is by controlling the color temperature of the image, which mainly affects the red and blue channels, and sometimes also by controlling the intensity of the green channel for correcting magenta/green color casts.

If you can specify the color temperature of the source light of the photograph, you can use white balance to automatically adjust the color to a more neutral one. Color temperature of the source light affects an image in the following manner: if the photograph was taken under a high color temperature light, the image will look blueish; if it was taken under a low color temperature light, the image will look yellowish.

Using white balance, the photographer can reduce the color casts of lighting or create specific effects in the image. For instance, if an image was taken in a room under fluorescent light, the image will look blueish. In this case, the white balance should be used with a fluorescent preset so that the blue casts are removed and the image is adjusted to something more similar to what the photographer was perceiving at the scene. Also, the photographer can change the temperature to create artistic shots, showing a scene with different colors compared to what an observer would see in the scene. Using warmer colors such as red, orange, or yellow will produce warmth and comfort feelings. Colder colors such as blue or purple can produce images that evoke calmness or sadness.

Many light sources produce color casts that you can adjust using mainly the color temperature. Although, under some lighting conditions, small green/magenta color casts are produced. This is produced mostly by artificial lightning because they irradiate different parts of the light spectrum compared to natural sources of light. The intensity of the green channel, also referred to sometimes as tint, is used to fine-tune the green/magenta cast in the image. This is usually done after the color temperature is adjusted.

Adjusting White Balance with Gimp

If you only have a digital image, and not the raw data, a specific white balance has already been selected to it. The **jpg** file format has less resolution than raw data, only 8 bits per channel, meaning that some information is lost (raw images usually have at least 10 bits per channel after demosaicing). This means that white balance will not be as effective as when working with raw data. Nevertheless, you can use Gimp to automatically adjust the white balance of your photograph. In Gimp, open the image that you want to process and select Colors → Auto → White Balance. This will automatically adjust the colors of the image. If you want more control over the image, you can select Colors → Levels. You can then select Auto to achieve the automatic white balance, or select any of the three eyedroppers as shown in Figure 4-1. You can choose a black, gray, or white eyedropper. Then, you just need to click on a black, gray, or white point in the image and Gimp will automatically adjust the rest of the image taking that point as the reference.

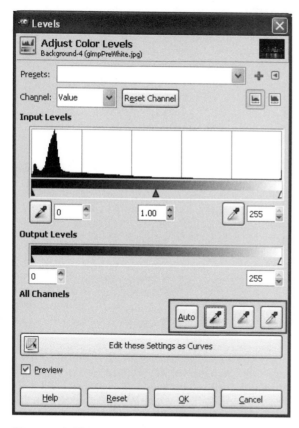

Figure 4-1. The automatic section of the Levels dialog box from Gimp. Note how there is a large portion of the histogram not being used. In this case, you should move the right triangle to the left to produce a more vivid image.

You can always take a look at what the automatic correction is doing. After you press the Auto button, just select any color channel and you will see how the arrows are changed to another position. This position is calculated so that they cover most of the pixels of the image in the reduced range (the portion that lies between the left and the right arrows), as shown in Figure 4-2.

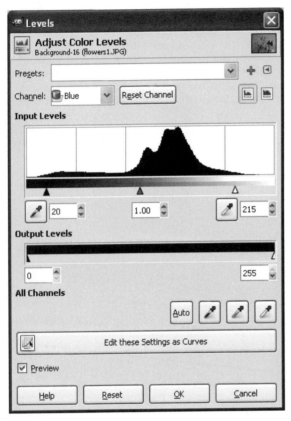

Figure 4-2. You can see the effect of the Auto button; the left and right arrows are moved to select most of the pixels shown in the histogram.

If you need more control over the colors of your image, you have plenty of options in the Levels dialog box, as you can see in Figure 4-6. Let's go through them step by step. The first option that you have is to select a Preset. This allows you to select any previous settings that you have saved before so that you don't have to remember how you achieved a specific effect. For saving your current level settings into a preset, you only need to click on the little plus sign and give it a name. It will immediately be added to the preset lists. You can change the settings for exploring and then go back to previous settings by just loading it from Presets.

The next option available is to select the color channel you will be working on. Every setting on this dialog box is tied to a specific color channel. If you change the color channel, the values for that channel will be loaded. You may think of this channel selection as a tabbed interface where you can select which tab you are working on at the moment. The color channel options are Value, Red, Green, Blue, and

Alpha. Value allows you to change the three color channels at the same time. The next three channels are the RGB standard colors. Finally, Alpha channel is used to control transparencies in the image. For photographs, you will most likely not be use the Alpha channel. Next to the channel selector is a Reset Channel button. If you click on it, all the default values will be loaded for the current channel.

Under Input Levels, there is a histogram of the current color channel. The left side represents low intensity (that is, shadows under the Value channel) while the right side represents high intensity (that is, highlights under the Value channel). The actual values of the pixels of the channel are used for drawing the histogram. You can see how the values of the current channel are distributed along the intensity line, from 0 to 255. The histogram is constructed by Gimp by looking at the image and asking: in this specific channel, how many of these values are 0? The answer to that question is the height of the curve in the left-most part of the histogram. Then, it continues asking for higher values and drawing the curve, until it reaches 255. The answer to how many values are 255 is the height of the curve at the right-most part of the histogram.

Now that you understand how histograms work, you can start changing the settings. There are three triangles under the intensity line: one on the left, one on the middle, and one on the right. They define the minimum and maximum values of that particular channel, as well as how balanced the current color channel is. The triangle on the left defines the minimum intensity for the channel. As you may think, by default it is 0. But what happens if your color channel doesn't have any value lower than 100? It means that you are wasting color depth on nonexistent values. This produces washed out images, with less saturated colors. For solving that, you can increase the minimum intensity to 100 so that you use your color depth in a better way. The same is true for the opposite side. What if your current color channel goes up to only 200? It means that you are also losing color depth in nonexistent values. As before, you can move the right triangle to 200 so that your maximum intensity matches the maximum intensity in that color channel. So now you can control how vivid your colors look, but what about the middle triangle? What does it do? It allows you to control how balanced, or how much tint of the current color the image will have. Its position is relative to the minimum and maximum triangles. If it is in the center of them, the tint of the color will remain the same. If you move the middle triangle to the left, it will make the current color channel more intense. If you move it to the right, it will make it less intense, meaning that the complementary color will be more intense. The complementary colors are the ones that are totally opposite in hue. Some of the most common ones are Red-Cyan, Green-Magenta, and Blue-Yellow. Therefore, if you move the middle slider to the right, you will be balancing the color towards the complementary color of the current color channel. For example, if you are in the Red channel, moving the slider to the left will add red tones to the image, while moving it to the right will add Cyan tones. The same holds true for the other color channels.

The next option that you have available is the Output Levels. This allows you to force all the values of the current channel to be inside the desired range. This basically reduces the contrast of the current channel to the one selected. Moving the left triangle to the right will increase the minimum value for that channel, while moving the right triangle to the left will reduce the maximum value for that channel. For example, if you have the Red channel selected, moving the left slider to the right will add red hues to your image, while moving the right triangle to the left will add cyan hues to it.

By using the Levels dialog box, you can manually remove any color casts on your images by just applying the complementary color to the image. Also, you can add any type of color casts to your images. Depending on the colors you add, you can set different moods for your image. For example, you can add red or yellow for giving a warmth effect to the image. On those types of images, you may also decrease the contrast of the colors to add a dreamy look. For generating very vibrantly colored images, you should move the left and right triangles of the input levels section under each color channel so that they cover a smaller section of the histogram, making your colors more alive.

Adjusting Color Balance with Gimp

There is also another tool for adjusting white balance in Gimp, called Color Balance. The nice thing about the Color Balance tool is that it allows you to make changes in different ranges of the image—shadows, midtones, and highlights—while the Levels tool only allows you to make changes in the complete range of the image. Keep in mind that if you don't need to make such detailed white balance correction, it is easier to just move the middle triangle for each color channel in the Levels dialog box. If you want to correct white balance differently, in shadows and highlights for example, you should use the Color Balance tool.

You can access the Color Balance tool by going into Colors → Color Balance. A dialog box similar to the one presented in Figure 4-3 should appear.

Let's review what options this dialog box offers. First, it allows you to save and load presets, similar to the Levels dialog box. Then, it gives you the options for which specific range you will be making changes to. You can make changes to the darkest parts of the image (Shadows), the brightest parts (Highlights), and everything in between (Midtones). There is an Adjust Color Levels section that presents you three sliders, one for each color balance. This works similar to the middle triangle in the Levels dialog box. If you move each slider to a side, it will add a cast of that color to the image. If you move it to the other side, it will add a cast of the complementary color. You can always go back to the default settings of the current range by pressing the Reset Range button. There is also a Preserve luminosity check box. When it is checked, the resulting pixels are scaled so that the original brightest pixel maintains its value. In practice, this means that when this option is checked, you will generate an image that has a similar brightness than the original. If it is not checked, the overall brightness may change. Finally, there is a Preview checkbox. When it is checked, you can immediately see the changes you have made in the image, which is really useful.

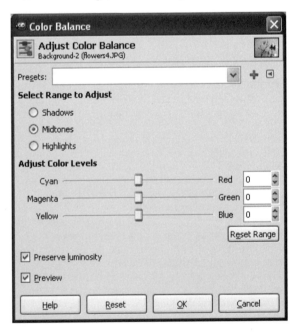

Figure 4-3. This image shows the options of Gimp's Color Balance dialog box.

Brightness and Contrast

Brightness and contrast are basic parameters that allow changing how the light is represented in the image.

Brightness controls the total amount of light present in the scene. Increasing it produces an overall lighter image, and decreasing it, an overall darker image.

Contrast is how far apart the darkest shadow and the brightest light are represented in the image. Increasing it results in darker shadows and brighter lights, obtaining a large visual separation between dark and light areas in the image; decreasing it makes shadows brighter and lights darker, resulting in a more uniform image.

In Gimp, you can access the Brightness and Contrast controls by selecting Colors → Brightness-Contrast. In the dialog box that appears (see Figure 4-4), you can increase or decrease both the brightness and the contrast of the image.

Figure 4-4. *This image shows the Brightness-Contrast dialog box. It allows you to easily change the brightness and contrast with only two sliders. If you want more control, you can click on Edit these Settings as Levels to open the Levels dialog box.*

If you want to make automatic changes, you can go to the Colors menu, then select Auto and after that, you can select Equalize for an automatic Contrast adjustment or Normalize for an automatic Brightness adjustment. The Gimp uses the histogram to calculate where to put the sliders for the automatic adjustments, as explained in the previous section.

The Brightness-Contrast dialog box is nothing more than a simplified version of the Levels dialog box that you are already familiar with.

The first slider, Brightness, allows you to move from -127 to 127. Smaller values produce darker images, while larger values produce brighter ones. Let's see how this really works. If you select a positive number, let's say 50, and then click on the *Edit these Settings as Levels* button, you will see that, under the *Value* channel, in the *Output Levels* section, the left arrow was moved up to 50 (Figure 4-5). The same is true for negative brightness, only that the value is subtracted from the right-most triangle. When the left-most triangle of the output section is moved to the right, it means that you are increasing the value of the blackest black. This means that the shadows will become brighter. On the other side, when the right-most triangle is moved to the left, you are decreasing the value of the whitest whites; therefore, the highlights will be darker

The second slider, Contrast, gives you the same range as the Brightness slider, -127 to 127. In the case of Contrast, you control how far apart the blackest black and the whitest whites are. When you increase the contrast, the effect is the same as if you would have reduced the range of the Input Levels in the Levels dialog box. As I explained in the previous section, reducing this range increases the contrast of the image. When you decrease the contrast, the effect is equal to reducing the range in the Output Levels in the Levels dialog box. This is because when the output range is shorter, the lowest values will be closer to the highest values; therefore, there will be less contrast (see Figure 4-6).

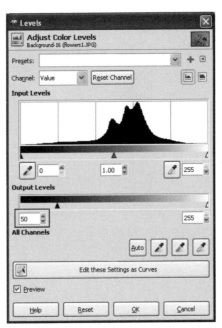

Figure 4-5. *The Brightness slider directly affects the left-most triangle of the Output Levels in the Levels dialog box. Likewise, if you select a negative brightness, the right-most triangle will be moved to the left by the same amount.*

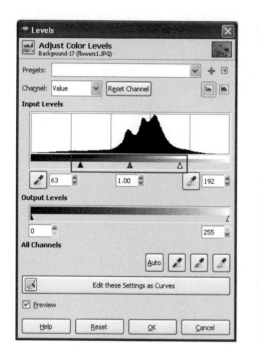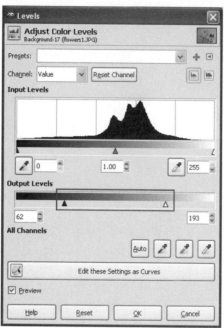

Figure 4-6. *To the left, you can see the effect of increasing the contrast of the image using the Brightness-Contrast dialog box, while on the right, you can see the effects of decreasing it.*

Figure 4-7 shows an example of an image that has low contrast and brightness.

Figure 4-7. An image with poor lighting and low contrast

For fixing this image, I will use the Brightness-Contrast dialog box. This dialog box is especially useful for making quick corrections. In this case, I used the settings shown in Figure 4-8.

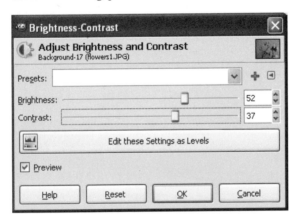

Figure 4-8. This image shows the settings used to correct the previous photo.

Figure 4-9 shows the results.

Figure 4-9. This is the result of correcting the image with the Brightness-Contrast dialog box.

Hue and Saturation

In the HSL color space, *hue* represents a color as humans would think, such as red or blue, for example. *Saturation* represents how intense that color is and *lightness* represents the intensity of light. Using hue and saturation, you can change how the colors look. Normally, the base color (hue) is correctly set in the image, but in some shots, the colors do not look as bright or intense as they were in the scene. By increasing saturation, colors can come alive.

You can access the Hue-Saturation dialog box in Gimp by selecting Colors → Hue-Saturation. This will open the Hue-Saturation dialog for box adjusting hue, saturation, and lightness, as shown in Figure 4-10.

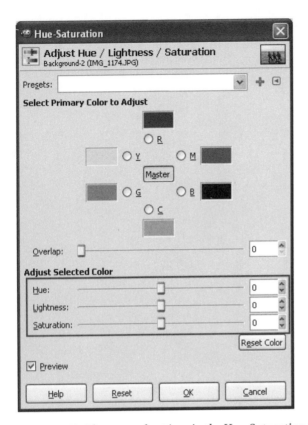

Figure 4-10. The manual settings in the Hue-Saturation dialog box

In this dialog box, you can change how colors look in your image. First, you have to select the current color, the one whose appearance you will be changing , and then move the sliders to change how it looks.

The first option that you have is to save or load presets, which work the same as the presets for the Levels dialog box; pick a previously saved one from the combo box, or save a new one by pressing the plus (+) sign. Then, you are given the option to pick the primary color to adjust. You can select any color that you want to change; you have the common red (R), green (G), and blue (B) ones and their complementary colors, cyan (C), magenta (M), and yellow (Y). The Master button in the center allows you to select all the colors at the same time.

Once you have selected a specific color, you can change any of the three sliders: hue, lightness, and saturation. Note that next to each color is a preview of the new color it will become when the settings are applied. This is why there are also text labels (R, G, B, C, M, and Y) so that when you change how a color looks, you still know which one it was in the beginning. Okay, let's review the settings:

- *Hue* defines the tint of the specific color; for example, red, blue, and green are three different hue values. Select, for example, the red color and move the hue slider. You will see how the red color starts changing into other colors such as green, blue, yellow, and so on. You can use this to change the color of an object in the image. You can always go back to the default settings by just clicking on the Reset Color button.

- The *lightness* slider allows you to change how light or dark you want that specific color to be in the image. Think of it like adding black to your color if you move the slider to the left and adding white to your color if you move the slider to the right.

- Finally, *saturation* allows you to define how vibrant is your color. This means that it can go from grayscale or very washed out color to a very vibrant or intense color.

As an example, I will show you how to change the colors of the flowers I showed you earlier. Since they mostly have a magenta/reddish color, I will select and change only those two colors, as shown in Figure 4-11.

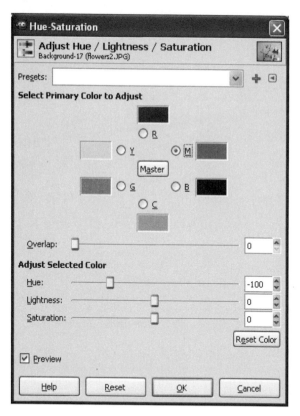

Figure 4-11. You can see how the new hues are presented in the Hue-Saturation dialog box. The text labels remain the same, but the color preview window changes to show the new values for every specific color.

The effect of changing the hue of the red and magenta colors is that anything in the image that had either of those colors are now redefined to be the new colors. In this particular case, the flowers will change from a magenta/reddish color to a blueish color. Note that the sticks also present a little change in color, due to the fact that they have some red components. You can easily fix this by only selecting the flowers with any selection tool before applying the color change.

As another example, I will show you how to make the colors of the plant more vibrant, since they are washed out. For this, you only need to change the saturation slider, since you want to maintain the original hues and lightness. Open the Hue–Saturation dialog box, select Master, and move the Saturation slider all the way up to 100, as shown in Figure 4-12.

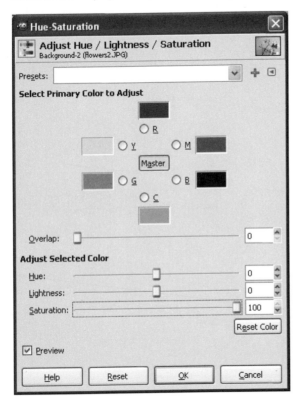

Figure 4-12. A suggested setting for boosting the colors of your images

The resulting image will show a much more vibrant image with more saturated colors. You could also specify individual saturations for each color if you want to highlight some colors more than others.

You also have an option for automatic saturation enhancement. You only need to go to Colors → Auto → Color Enhance. Gimp will internally transform the image into the HSV color space, stretch the saturation channel to the maximum possible range, and finally convert the image back to RGB. The result will be an image with much more vibrant colors.

Grayscale

A grayscale image has only information about intensity of light, not the color of it. There are many ways to generate grayscale, often incorrectly named black and white, images. Color images usually have three channels, so you have to mix that information into just one channel, storing intensity information and losing the color information.

The most common color space in digital images is RGB, which means that the intensity of the red, green, and blue parts of the image is stored independently. If you use the average of those three channels, you will get a grayscale version of the image.

Another option is to change the color space of the image to one that represents light or brightness in a single channel and then choose that channel as the grayscale image. One of those color spaces is HSL (Hue, Saturation, and Lightness). First, converting the RGB color space to HSL and then choosing the L produces a grayscale image of the scene that is in general better than just taking the average of the RGB channels.

Lab (Luminosity, channel a, and channel b) is a more complex color space designed based on how humans perceive color and luminosity. As before, you convert the image to the Lab color space and then select only the Luminosity channel to generate a grayscale image.

If you want to create a grayscale image that is very similar to what humans perceive as light intensity, you should use the Luminosity channel of the Lab color space, as it was specially designed for that purpose.

Gimp offers all of these three options. Open the color image that you want to convert to grayscale and select Color → Desaturate. If you are wondering about the name of this command, it is because grayscale is the opposite of a saturated color. Here, a dialog box with the three previously explained options are presented (Figure 4-13). Lightness refers to the HSL conversion, Luminosity to the Lab conversion, and Average uses the average of the RGB channels.

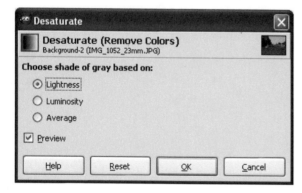

Figure 4-13. The Desaturate dialog box, with the three options for creating the grayscale image

Curves

The most general way to adjust color in a digital image in Gimp is by using the Curves tool. With Curves, every single color in the image is mapped to a new one. By selecting specific curves, you can invert the colors of the image; increase or decrease brightness, contrast, saturation; remove color casts; and many more things. It is a very powerful tool, but you need to know what you are doing to use it properly. In this section, I will show you how to use it.

Open the Curves dialog box by selecting Colors → Curves. Similar to the Levels tool, when you are using the Curves tool, you are changing one channel at a time. This channel can be Value, which is the overall intensity of the image (R, G, and B selected at the same time), or any specific color channel. You can reset to the default settings on the current channel any time by just clicking the Reset Channel button. Also, you can load presets by selecting them from the drop-down menu or save your current settings to a preset by clicking on the plus (+) sign.

The Curves tool shows you the histogram of the image, and initially a linear curve that connects the inputs with the outputs without any change, as shown in Figure 4-14.

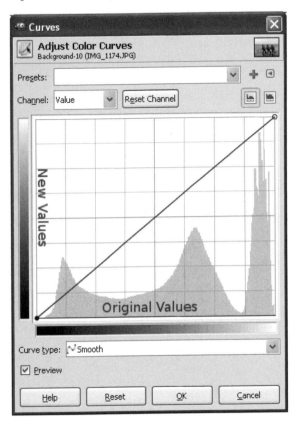

Figure 4-14. This is the Curves dialog box. The horizontal axis shows the original values of the current channel, while the vertical axis shows the new values for the current channel. Initially, there is a linear curve that connects the input values with the same output values.

It is very important for you to understand what the curve part of the dialog box means. First, let's review what the histogram means. On the current channel, the image has different values inside the 0-255 range. These values can represent different things; for example, if the current channel is Value, they would represent the brightness of each pixel. Darker pixels will have lower values, closer to zero, while brighter pixels will have higher values, closer to 255. On the other hand, if the channel selected is Red, these values would represent the intensity of that color of each pixel. Values closer to 0 represent that those pixels do not have much red in its color, while values closer to 255 represent that those pixels have a large red component. Given a specific channel, Gimp counts how many of those values are 0, 1, 2, and so on until 255. With those numbers, it draws a graph. This graph is the histogram presented in the Curves dialog box. Therefore, by just looking at the horizontal axis and the histogram, you can see how many shadows or how many highlights an image has, depending on the height of the histogram in those areas.

Now that you know what the histogram and the horizontal axis are, it is time to review the vertical axis. The vertical axis represents the new values that the current channel will have. This means that for each point in the horizontal axis (the current value), there is one point in the vertical axis (the new value). Take, for instance, the two points in Figure 4-22. The black point, which is on the left-most part of the horizontal axis, currently has a value of 0 (black) and it will have a new value of 0 as well, which is the lowest part of the vertical axis. The other point, which is in the right-most part of the horizontal axis, has a current value of 255 (white) and a new value of 255 as well, which is the top of the vertical axis. The same is true for all the other points in between; each one of them has their current value on the horizontal axis connected with the same value on the vertical axis. This means that the initial curve will maintain the image untouched. Now I will show you some of the effects that you can achieve with the Curves tool. Figure 4-15 shows the original image that the effects will be applied to.

Figure 4-15. This is the original image that is going to be used for showing the effects of the Curves tool.

As a first example, I will show you how to invert the colors of an image. To do this, you will need to drag each one of the two control points and move them to a new location. First, go to the black point (the one is the lower left part), click and drag it into the upper left part of the graph. Now go to the white point (the one in the upper right part), click and drag it into the lower right part of the graph. You should end up with something like Figure 4-16. Figure 4-17 shows the results on the image.

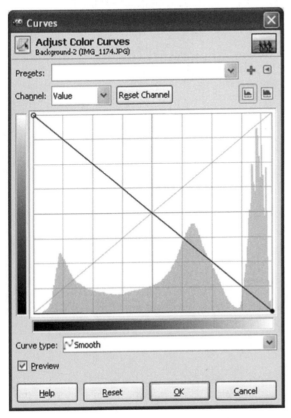

Figure 4-16. This image shows how to invert the colors of a photograph. Note how black in the horizontal axis is now connected to white in the vertical axis, and vice-versa.

Figure 4-17. This is the result of inverting the original image.

Now you need to learn how to add and remove control points. Control points allow you to change the curve in a smooth manner. You can add control points by just clicking on the curve. Click three times on the curve, in the positions shown in the Figure 4-18. This will add three control points: one for shadows, one for midtones, and one for highlights. You can drag control points to change the curve appearance. You can remove any extra point by just dragging it towards any side of the dialog box and releasing the button there.

Now that you have these three extra control points, you can control how the shadows, midtones, and highlights look in the picture. For example, if you move the shadows control point up, it means that the shadows will become brighter. If you move it down, you will darken the shadows. The same is true for the other two control points, you can increase or decrease the brightness of the midtones or the highlights as well by just dragging their respective control points up or down.

Let's now increase the contrast of the image. First, you need to think that increasing the contrast means that the shadows get darker and the highlights get brighter. As you already know, you can achieve this by just dragging two of the control points you previously created. First, move the shadows control point down for darkening them and then drag the highlights control point up to brighten them up. You will end up with something similar to Figure 4-19.

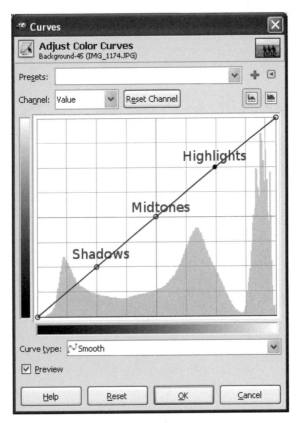

Figure 4-18. *This image shows how to add control points in specific positions for controlling shadows, midtones, and highlights.*

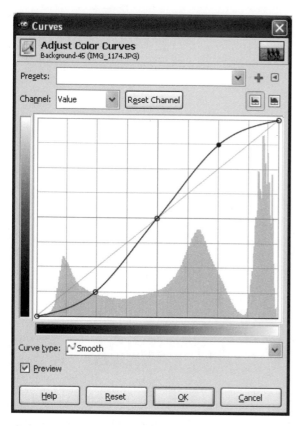

Figure 4-19. *This image shows how to increase the contrast of a photograph. Shadows are set to become darker (lower value), while highlights are set to become brighter (higher value).*

Figure 4-20 shows the results of increasing the contrast.

Figure 4-20. This is the result of increasing the contrast of the original image.

You can also do the opposite, decrease the contrast. As before, you can achieve this by just dragging the shadows and highlights control points to a new location. In this case, you need the shadows brighter and the highlights darker. Therefore, you need to move the shadows control point up and the highlights control point down. You should get something similar to Figure 4-21.

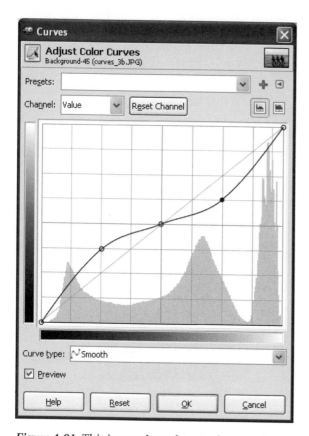

Figure 4-21. This image shows how to decrease the contrast of a photograph. Shadows are set to become brighter (higher value), while highlights are set to become darker (lower value).

Figure 4-22 shows the results of decreasing the contrast.

Figure 4-22. This is the result of decreasing the contrast of the original image.

If you drag the control points horizontally, it means that you are covering a larger or smaller range of shadows, midtones, or highlights on each case. For example, if you drag the shadows control point down and then you drag it to the right, as shown in Figure 4-23, it means that you will be darkening a larger range of shadows than you did before. Figure 4-24 shows where most of the shadows are darker. If you would have dragged the shadows control point to the left, a smaller range of shadows would have been darkened. So, moving the control points up or down brightens or darkens respectively the specific regions, depending on which control point is being dragged. On the other hand, dragging the control points horizontally enlarges or shortens the region it controls.

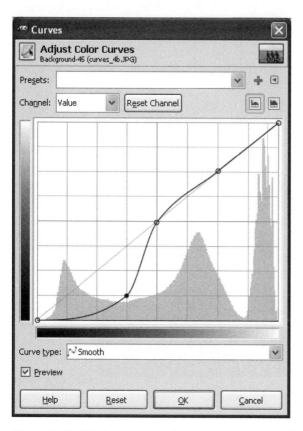

Figure 4-23. This image shows how dragging a control point horizontally changes the region it affects. In this case, the shadows control point was moved to the right, so it now affects a larger region than before. In the case of the highlights control point, it is the reverse; moving it to the left enlarges the region it affects.

Figure 4-24. *This image shows how a larger portion of the shadows become darker when moving the shadows control point to the right.*

As you can see, Curves is a very powerful tool that you can use to control the color of the image with great detail. At the same time, it is much more complex to use than the other tools. Therefore, I recommend that you start adjusting the colors of your images with the other tools and anytime you need more flexibility, you can start using this tool.

Summary

In this chapter, I showed you how to control the colors of your image. You are now able to correct the white balance of your images with great detail. Also, you are able to add any color cast to your photos so that they express some specific emotions. Another thing that you learned here is that you can enhance your images by increasing their contrast and brightness. You can also now edit your photographs so that they show more vibrant colors. Another thing that you are able to do now is to change the color of specific objects in your image as well as creating grayscale version of your images. Finally, you also learned how to use diverse tools in Gimp for color processing such as Levels, Color Balance, and Curves.

In the next Chapter, I will show you how to use some of the most popular filters, which allow you to greatly enhance your images.

CHAPTER 5

■ ■ ■

Filters

It all started with optical filters. For a long time, photographers have been attaching filters to their lenses so that they could have more control on the shots they capture. With the help of these filters, they can make changes to their images and create better photos. There are many types of optical filters, each one for a specific use. Some examples of them are color-correcting filters, infrared filters, neutral density filters, and many more. Once digital photography started, digital filters were created. A digital filter is basically a generic term for referring to a special mathematical operation applied to an image. Similar to optical filters, you can apply many operations to a digital image. Each one of them can produce very different results. Some of these operations are used to increase or decrease the sharpness of the image; others are used to remove unwanted noise in the image. There are many other usages, including artistic effects. A generic term that is commonly used to describe all of these operations is *filters*. In this chapter, I will show you some of the filters most commonly used in digital photography. The filters that I will show you are Blur, Sharpness, Noise Reduction, and a couple of Artistic filters. But first, I will show you how to select a specific region of the image so that you can apply the filter to it instead of the entire image.

Selecting a Region

Sometimes you may want to apply a filter only to a specific region, and not to the entire image. You can do that by first selecting the region using one of the many selection tools that Gimp offers, which are shown in Figure 5-1, and then applying the filter. Note that after selecting a region, any action such as a brush to paint, these filters, or any other editing tool will only occur within that selection until the selection is cleared. You can clear the selection by choosing Select → None.

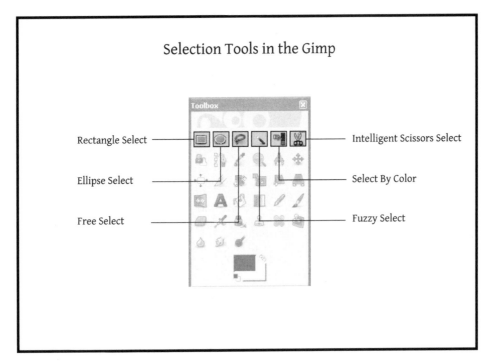

Figure 5-1. *Selection Tools available in Gimp*

Let's start with the simplest selection tool: Rectangle select.

Rectangle Select

This tool allows you to select any rectangular region of the image. You can start using this tool by just going to Tools → Selection Tools → Rectangle Select. You can also press the R key to access it, or click on its icon in the Toolbox, as shown in Figure 5-1.

For selecting a region, you only need to first click on the image where you want one corner of the rectangle and then move the mouse to where you want the other corner of the region to be. After you release the mouse, you will see a rectangular selection, as shown in Figure 5-2. You can move it around by dragging it and you can also resize it if you drag its sides or corners.

Figure 5-2. This image shows an example of the Rectangle Select tool. You can drag the sides of the rectangle to change its size as well as drag the rectangle itself to move it to another position.

Ellipse Select Tool

The next tool you can use is the Ellipse Select tool. This can be useful for selecting areas that are not rectangular, such as a head, an eye, or a ball, for example. It is next to the Rectangle Select Tool in the Toolbox. You can click its icon there to activate it, as shown in Figure 5-1. Also, you can press the E key or go to Tools → Selection Tools → Ellipse Select.

This tool works exactly the same as the Rectangle Select tool; the only difference is that the region that you select is the ellipse that fits into the rectangle you created. You can change the size and position of the elliptical region by dragging the rectangle where it lies, as shown in Figure 5-3.

Figure 5-3. This image shows an example of using of the Ellipse Select tool. Note how there is a rectangle that encompasses the selection ellipse. You can edit the ellipse by changing this rectangle.

Free Select Tool

The Free Select tool allows you to freely draw the region you want to select with your mouse. This is useful for regions that cannot be represented easily by rectangles or ellipses. This is particularly common when you need to select a foreground object. You can access this tool by pressing the F key, or by going into Tools → Selection Tools → Free Select. Also, you can click on its icon on the Toolbox window to activate it, as shown in Figure 5-1.

To select a region with this tool, you only need to click and move your mouse around the area of the image you want to select, as shown in Figure 5-4, until you reach the starting point, then release the mouse button. This way, you close the region and it gets selected. You can also make the selection step-by-step. Just click on the initial point of your region and continue clicking along the border of the region you want to select. The tool will connect the previous point with the current one using a straight line. To finish the selection, just click on the starting point again and the area will be selected.

Figure 5-4. This image shows an example of using the Free Selection tool.

Fuzzy Select Tool

This tool allows you to select contiguous areas that have a similar intensity. It is very useful for selecting objects with clearly defined borders. You can access this tool by clicking on its icon in the Toolbox, as shown in Figure 5-1, pressing U, or by going into Tools → Selection Tools → Fuzzy Select.

You can select a region by just clicking on a specific pixel in the image. The selection starts including this first pixel. Then, the tool will start growing the selection including only the pixels that are close and with a similar intensity. You can control how sensitive the tool is by changing its Threshold setting under the Toolbox window. The default value is 15. This means that if the difference in intensity between the first pixel and its neighbor is less than 15, it will be included in the selection. Considering that both values can go from 0 to 255, a difference of 15 represents about 6%, or $1/17^{th}$. The internal process of creating the selection is repeated until no other pixel can be added. You can change the Threshold from 0 to 255, where 0 means that it will only select pixels that are exactly the same color (difference equals 0) and 255 means that it will select all the pixels of the image. In the example shown in Figure 5-5, I used 60 as the threshold.

Figure 5-5. *This image shows the result of using the Fuzzy Select tool. After I clicked on one black pixel, all the contiguous black pixels were selected. Note that the other two black regions of the image that are not connected with the original pixel are not selected.*

You can also change the Threshold interactively. Click on the first pixel that you want to select, and while maintaining the button pressed, move the mouse right to increase the Threshold and left to decrease it. You can also achieve this by moving the mouse down or up, respectively. Once you get the desired region, release the button and it will be selected.

Select By Color

The Select by Color tool is almost the same as the Fuzzy Select tool. The main difference is that it selects all the pixels of the image with similar intensity, not just the ones that are physically close as the Fuzzy Select tool does. You can access this tool by clicking on its icon in the Toolbox, as shown in Figure 5-1, pressing Shift+O, or by going into Tools → Select → By Color Select.

You can see an example of this tool in Figure 5-6.

Figure 5-6. This image shows the result of using the Select by Color tool. After I clicked on one black pixel, all the black pixels of the image were selected. Note that by using this tool, all the pixels of the image with a similar intensity, contiguous or not, are selected.

Intelligent Scissors Select Tool

The Intelligent Scissors Select tool enables you to select regions easily by considering the contents of the image. You only need to outline the region you want to select by clicking on its border. You can access this tool by clicking on its icon in the Toolbox window, as shown in Figure 5-1, or by pressing the I key. You can also access it by going into Tools → select → Intelligent Scissors.

Start by clicking on the border of the region you want to select. Continue clicking along the border of the region. The tool connects the previous point with the current one based on the contents of the image instead of just a straight line. You can see this effect in Figure 5-7. You can drag any point (except for the first and last ones) to adjust the region. Once you get to the finish, make sure that you click on the first point so that the region is now closed. After you click on the first (last) point, you can drag any of the points to make the final adjustments. At this time, you can still add points; you only need to click on the border line of the region. Once you are ready, just click inside the region and it will be selected.

Figure 5-7. *This image shows how the Intelligent Scissors Select tool connects the previous point with the current one based on the contents of the image.*

Adding and Removing Regions

Using any of the previously discussed tools, you can add regions to or remove them from your currently selected area. You only need to know that by holding the Shift key, you are adding a region to your selection and that by holding the Control key, you are removing a region from it. Just make the selection with any tool while you hold any of those two keys and the region will be added or subtracted from the current selection. This allows you to make complex selections based on simpler regions. Note that when you press any of these keys, a plus or a minus sign is added to the selection tool cursor.

Editing the Selection

Once you have selected a region, you can make global changes to it. Some of the most useful ones are Grow, Shrink, Invert, and Feather. Grow allows you to make your selection larger by any number of pixels. You can access it by going to Select → Grow. There, you can adjust the number of pixels by which you want your selection to grow. Shrink is the opposite of Grow; it allows you to make your selection smaller by any number of pixels. You can access it by going to Select → Shrink. There, you can adjust the number of pixels by which you want your selection to shrink. You can Invert your selection any time by going to Selection → Invert. This will select the background instead of the foreground, or vice versa. It is very useful when the opposite selection is very complicated to make, so you can first select the easier one and then invert it. Another useful change you can make to your selection is Feather. This makes a smooth transition between what is selected and what is not. This way, any changes you make in the selection are blended with the rest of the image. You can access this feature by going into Selection → Feather. A dialog box will appear asking for how many pixels you want to feather. The more pixels you put, the larger the transition from inside to outside the selected region will be. You can always remove the feather of a selection by going into Select → Sharpen.

Now that you are able to select any specific region of the image, I will start showing you the different filters that you can apply to your images. I'll start with Blur, which is a very commonly used filter.

Blur

Blur is a filter that diffuses the contents of the image, creating a softer photograph. This filter is commonly used to soften cluttered backgrounds so that the focus of the image remains only on the main subject. It is also used to create a sense of motion of the subject, to minimize the effect of harsh borders, and to add artistic effects.

Blur is naturally produced by many factors. For example, by controlling the field of view, the photographer can blur the background. With a long exposure time, moving objects appear blurred on the photograph. And the most common cause of blur for beginners is movement of the camera itself.

You can produce digital blur in post processing. For example, for emulating the effect of a blurred background with controlled field of view, you need to first select the background in the image and then apply blur only on that part. This allows the main subject to remain sharp, while the cluttered background gets blurred. You can apply other types of blur so that, for example, the subject seems to be moving fast.

There are many types of blur filters, although I will show you some of the most common ones: Simple Blur, Gaussian Blur, Motion Blur, and Pixelize.

Simple Blur

Gimp offers a quick blur filter that does not need any parameters. This method calculates, for every pixel of the image, the average of its neighboring pixels. That way, for each channel, a new value is calculated pixel by pixel using the average of their adjacent pixels. This means that the difference between the pixels gets smaller every time this filter is executed. Because of these simple calculations, it is a very fast method. On the other hand, it does not provide many options to the photographer. Because the pixel neighborhood is fixed, small images get very blurred, while the blur effect is almost not noticeable on large images. If you are using a large image, such as the full-resolution image from a digital camera, it is better to use another approach, such as the Gaussian Blur where you can control how much blur you want. On the other hand, if you only want to add a quick and small amount of blur, you can use this filter. Also, you can apply it multiple times so that the image gets blurrier every time. In Gimp, you can access this Simple Blur by opening your image and going to the Filters → Blur → Blur. You can see an example of this type of Blur in Figure 5-8. It shows a skin close up. You can see how the skin imperfections are lost, generating a smoother image. This is usually done to soften the skin of people. It can also be done to reduce the noise or graininess in the images.

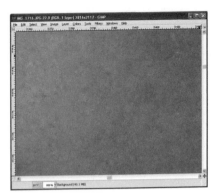 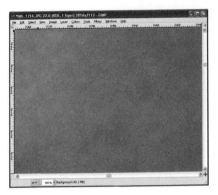

Figure 5-8. This image shows a person's skin close up. The left image shows the original, while the right image shows it after applying Blur. You can see that the result is a softer skin.

Gaussian Blur

The Gaussian Blur uses a specific mathematical that which has its maximum value in the center and slowly decreases to the sides (see Figure 5-9). This produces a propagation of the pixel values to their neighbors. The visual effect is that neighbor pixels are mixed together, producing a smoother image. For example, if there is an abrupt change in colors, we are able to see a sharp division between them, as Figures 5-10 shows. If we apply Gaussian Blur to it, the border becomes less evident. In a real-world photograph, you can see that the fine details of the image are lost, producing a much softer image than the original, as shown in Figures 5-11 and 5-12. You can use Gaussian Blur when the region that you want to Blur is larger or when you want more control.

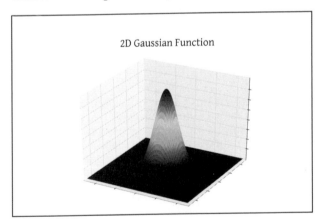

Figure 5-9. An example of a Gaussian Function. This is the type of function used in the Gaussian Blur filter. It shows the weight or importance of the color of a pixel around the subject pixel to be used to influence the alteration of the subject.

Figure 5-10. *This image depicts a simple example of harsh borders. Note how visible the dividing line is in the left image. After applying a Gaussian blur, the dividing line is much less noticeable (right image).*

Figure 5-11. *This image shows the original photograph of a real-world scene. Note that the image is sharp and you can see details of the face of the subject .*

Figure 5-12. This image shows the result of a Gaussian Blur applied to the previous image. Note how the details are lost and the image is much softer, especially in the hair and the eyes.

In Gimp, you can access the Gaussian Blur by opening the image that you want to edit and selecting Filters → Blur → Gaussian Blur.

In the Gaussian Blur dialog box (Figure 5-13), you can select the blur radius and the method to be used. The *blur radius* represents the shape of the Gaussian Function and you can think of it as the intensity of the effect; higher values produce large amounts of blurriness, while lower values produce slight blurriness in the image. There are two possible implementation methods from which to choose: Infinite Impulse Response (IIR) and Run-Length Encoding (RLE). It's not important exactly how these methods differ, but both of them produce the exact same final results, although in some cases, depending on the image, one method can be faster than the other. RLE is faster for images that have large areas with the exact same color, such as diagrams, line art, and so forth. On the other hand, IIR is faster for real-world images that present many color changes. For real-world images, such as photographs, it is better to use IIR instead of RLE.

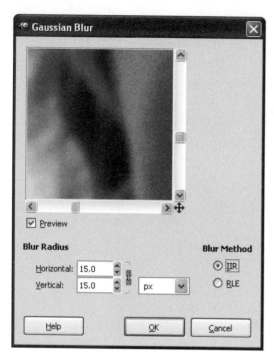

Figure 5-13. This image shows the Gaussian Blur dialog box in Gimp.

Motion Blur

The Motion Blur filter emulates the effect of taking a photograph of moving objects. Adding this type of Blur can add the illusion that the objects in the image were moving when in reality they were not.

You can access the Motion Blur filter in Gimp by going into Filters → Blur → Motion Blur. A dialog box will appear asking for the Amount and the Direction of the effect, similar to the one shown in Figure 5-14. The angle tells Gimp in which direction you want to move the object. You can see the effect in real-time in the preview window. As a guide, 180 degrees means that the object will be moving to the right, whereas 0 and 360 means that the object will be moving to the left. 90 degrees means that the object will move up, whereas 270 degrees means that the object will move down. The amount of the effect is the magnitude of the movement. Higher numbers mean that the object will be moved farther away in the selected direction. The other options, Radial and Zoom, allow you to make more complex distortions. For emulating general movement of solid objects, you can just use the linear option and ignore the rest.

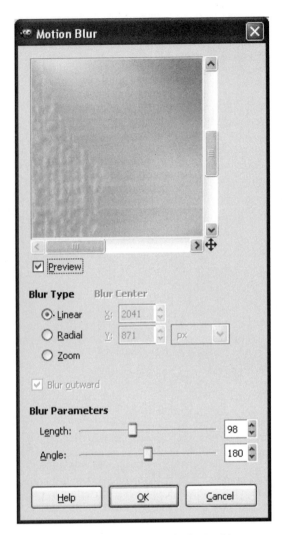

Figure 5-14. The Motion Blur dialog in Gimp

You can see an example of using this tool in Figure 5-15. It seems like the white queen is moving to the right, when in fact it was perfectly still. I used the Intelligent Scissors to select the object, then added 30 pixels of feather so that the effect can blend. Finally, I chose a Motion Blur with 98 in Length and 180 in Angle (movement to the right, as opposed to 0, which is to the left and everything in between).

Figure 5-15. This image shows the white queen moving to the right, while it was shot perfectly still. This is the result of applying linear motion blur with an angle of 180 degrees and an amount of 98.

Pixelize

The Pixelize blur simulates reducing the resolution of the image. The visual effect is similar to not having enough resolution; pixels, or color blocks, are visible to the human eye. This filter is mostly used for censoring or hiding any type of information in the image, as shown in Figure 5-15.

Figure 5-16. The left image shows the original photograph, while the right image shows the result of applying the Pixelize filter to the number on the floor.

You can access this filter by going into Filters → Blur → Pixelize. A dialog box will appear with a preview window and the size of the effect, as shown in Figure 5-17. The larger the values you input, the more pixelized the resulting image will be. You can set a different number for horizontal and vertical pixilation by clicking the chain icon, although in general I would recommend that you just use the same number for both since it looks better.

Figure 5-17. This image shows the dialog box for the Pixelize filter in Gimp. You should increase the pixel width and height until you don't recognize the data in the image.

Sharpness

Sharpness is one of the most popular filters in digital photography. This is because, if used correctly, it greatly enhances the image, highlighting details and giving well-defined edges to the objects of the scene. In photographic terms, it increases the *acutance* of the image.

Usually, consumer digital cameras produce a soft image with poor borders because of lack of resolution or optical problems. You can solve this partially by using the Sharpness filter. This filter exaggerates the contrast along the edges present in the photograph, therefore creating the illusion that the image is actually sharper than it was before. You can see an example of this in Figure 5-18.

Figure 5-18. The right image shows the result of the Unsharp Mask over the left image. The contrast is enhanced in the edge, giving the illusion of a sharper image.

I recommend that you use some form of this filter on every photograph that you take; in almost all the cases, your images will look better. Gimp offers two versions of this filter, Sharpen and Unsharp Mask.

Sharpen

Sharpen is a very basic filter that allows you to increase the sharpness of the image with almost no inputs. You can access this filter by going into Filters → Enhance → Sharpen.

You only need to select the level of sharpness, from 1 to 99, where 1 is the lowest amount and 99 is the maximum level of sharpness. For regular photographs, you should start increasing this value from around 10 until before the image starts looking grainy.

Unsharp Mask

The most commonly used and powerful filter for sharpening has the rather confusing name of Unsharp Mask (USM). This method increases the contrast of the differences between the original image and a blurred version of it, accentuating the edges of the original image, increasing their contrast, and enhancing the details. Figure 5-20 shows the results of using this filter on the image in Figure 5-19.

The USM commonly provides photographers three parameters that they can use to control the final sharpness; Amount, Radius, and Threshold. *Amount* refers to the intensity of the effect; how much lighter the light parts and darker the dark parts of the edges will be. *Radius* defines the size of the Gaussian Blur to be applied, which can be thought of as the size of the edges to be enhanced; a small radius will enhance small details and a large radius, large details. *Threshold* is a setting used to prevent enhancing very small subtle edges such as noise or other non-important details in low contrast areas. You can increase this value to filter them out and still sharpen the other details.

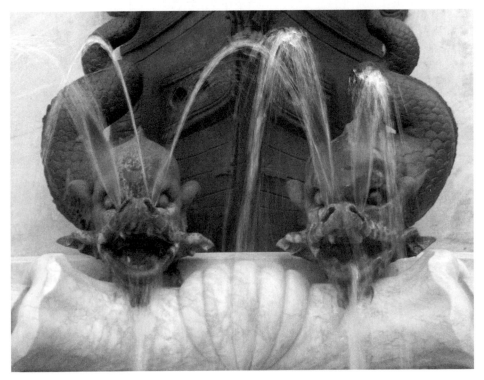

Figure 5-19. This image shows the original, unprocessed shot. Note how an overall soft or smooth look is present in the photograph.

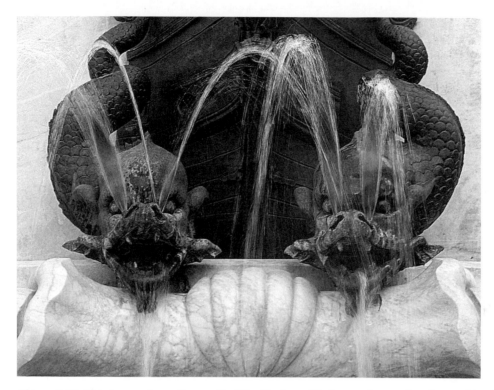

Figure 5-20. *This image shows the result of the Unsharp Mask over the previous image. Note how sharp the image looks now, highlighting the details of both the statue and water.*

Unsharp Mask gives you more flexibility than Sharpen with its three controls, Amount, Radius, and Threshold, which were previously explained. You can change these values and see the preview of a small area in real time.

To access Unsharp Mask, you need to open your image and select Filters → Enhance → Unsharp Mask. The Unsharp Mask dialog box is shown in Figure 5-21.

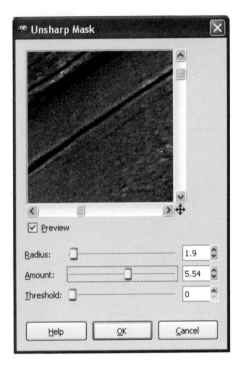

Figure 5-21. This image shows the Unsharp Mask dialog box in Gimp.

In normal conditions, the filter is applied to the three channels, R, G, and B. This sometimes may lead to very small changes in color. If you need the best results, you should apply the filter only to the Lightness channel. In order to do that, you need to first decompose the image into the Lab color space. Open the image and click Color → Components → Decompose. The Decompose dialog box is shown in Figure 5-22.

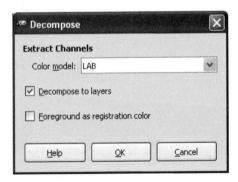

Figure 5-22. This image shows how to decompose an image into a different color space in Gimp. Note that Lab color space is selected.

After decomposing the image into the Lab color space, you need to select the Lightness channel (L) in the Layers window. You can do that by just clicking on the L layer, as Figure 5-23 shows.

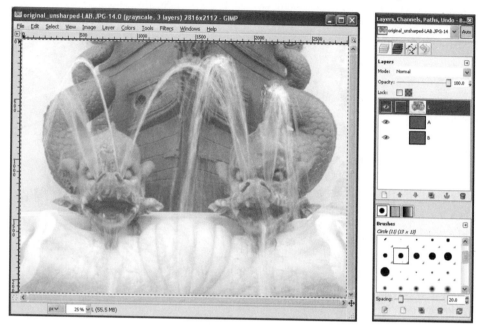

Figure 5-23. This image shows the result of the Lab decomposition. Note that Lightness channel is selected.

Now you can apply the Unsharp Mask filter to the Lightness channel of the Lab decomposed version of the image. After doing that, you can recompose the image by selecting Colors → Components → Recompose.

Noise Reduction

In digital images, random or odd colored pixels that do not represent the scene are called *noise*. Every digital camera produces some sort of noise in their images due to the use of digital sensors, which are not perfect. On top of that, in poor lighting conditions, photographers usually increase the ISO settings of the camera, increasing the levels of graininess in the image.

Noise degrades the overall quality of the image, giving it a non-professional look. Although, in general, when taking photographs under low lighting conditions, I recommend that you increase the ISO settings of your camera instead of changing other controls, such as increasing the exposure time, for example. This is because, as you will see next, you can reduce noise using filters in the computer much more easily than trying to fix an incorrectly exposed subject. This means that it is always better to have your objective correctly exposed with some noise rather than an image without noise of an incorrectly exposed objective.

There are different filters that can help us decrease the level of noise in images. One of the most popular filters for noise reduction is called Selective Gaussian Blur, and as the name suggests, it is based on the previously described Gaussian Blur. The key difference in this filter is that it only applies blur to specific areas of the image, not the entire image as the regular Gaussian Blur does. These specific areas have continuity in their intensity, or in other words, have a uniform color. By blurring only these specific areas, noise is reduced, preserving the edges of the objects. Figure 5-24 shows the effect of this filter.

Figure 5-24. This image shows the effect of noise reduction. On the left is the original image taken with ISO 800, presenting visible noise. On the right is the same image processed with Selective Gaussian Blur. Note how the noise is greatly reduced without decreasing the sharpness of the original image.

You can access this filter in Gimp by opening your image and selecting Filters → Blur → Selective Gaussian Blur.

There are two different parameters that you can control in the Selective Gaussian Blur filter. The first of them is the Blur radius. This option allows you to control the intensity of the effect. It works the same as in the regular Gaussian Blur; higher values will produce a blurrier image, removing more noise. The other option, maximum delta, refers to the threshold for selecting the areas that will be blurred. On one extreme, you can choose 255, which means that any difference between pixels is accepted for blurring. This would produce the same results as the regular Gaussian Blur, losing the details of the edges. On the other extreme, you can choose 0 as the maximum delta. This means that no pixel difference will be considered for blurring, obtaining the same original image. You need to find a number in between that gives you a good balance; if you choose a number lower than the ideal, you will leave noise in the image. On the other hand, if you choose a number higher than the ideal, you will blur some edges.

Artistic Filters

There are many artistic filters out there that change your images in every imaginable way; they can turn your image into a sphere or into a group of cubes, make it look cartoonish, add a three dimensional frame, make your images look old, and so on. In this section, I will show you a few examples of these filters.

Old Photo

Old printed photographs look different than new ones. They differ in color, sharpness, and many other characteristics. You can make your own photos look like they were taken many years ago. You can do this by processing the image in specific ways so that they appear to share the same characteristics of these old pictures. Figure 5-25 shows how this looks.

Figure 5-25. The left image shows the original photograph. On the right is the result of applying the old photo filter.

Gimp offers a filter that does exactly that, called Old Photo (Figure 5-26). You can access it from the Filters menu, under the Decor section.

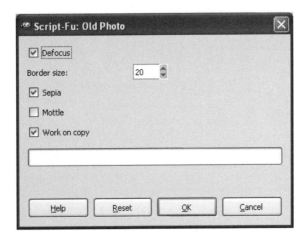

Figure 5-26. *The Old Photo dialog box in Gimp.*

On the Old Photo dialog box, you have a couple of options. Defocus allows you to apply a Gaussian Blur to the image so that it loses focus a little bit, which adds to the old photo effect. The Sepia option allows you to apply the typical brownish color of old photographs to your image. When Mottle is checked, it adds graininess to your image, which can also add to the effect of an old photo. Work on copy means that it will first create a copy of your current image and transform that copy into an old photo while keeping your original intact.

Softglow

This filter searches for the brightest parts of the image and make them even brighter. The visual effect of this filter is that the image appears to be lightened with a soft glow. In some cases, it gives the image a feeling of romance, magic, or dreaminess. It is often used in wedding or family portraits as well as in some landscapes. Figure 5-27 shows the effects of this filter.

Figure 5-27. *The left image is the original photograph. The right image shows the result of applying the Softglow filter.*

You can access this filter in Gimp through Filters → Artistic → Softglow.

You can adjust the Glow radius, Brightness, and Sharpness of the filter, as Figure 5-28 shows. The first parameter, Glow radius, controls how intense the effect will be in the image. The second parameter, Brightness, controls how bright the brightest parts of the image will be. Finally, the Sharpness parameter controls how defined or diffused the glow effect will be.

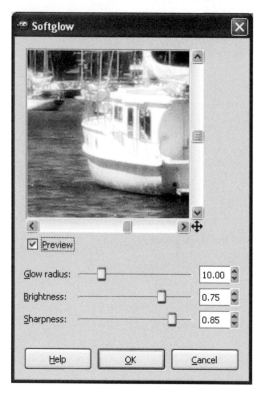

Figure 5-28. This image shows the Softglow dialog box in Gimp.

Summary

In this chapter, you learned how to enhance your images by sharpening them and reducing their noise. Also, you learned how to apply blur to create different effects, such as smoothing skin, censoring some regions by pixelating them, and creating the illusion of movement of your objects by using the Motion Blur. In addition, you also learned about a few of artistic filters for special shots.

In the next chapter, I will show you how to retouch your images so that you can fix small problems in your images, such as red eyes and more.

CHAPTER 6

Photo Retouching

Photo retouching is making small changes to your image so that you can fix some problems it has. From time to time, one can be in a situation where even if you have taken a great photograph, something is wrong about it; suddenly a leaf moved and appeared in the corner of your unique shot; your friend's eyes appeared glowing red in the image; the metadata, which is the information about your photograph, was lost after processing the image with some editor; and so forth. These are some of the occasions where photo retouching comes into play: removing unwanted objects, red-eye removal, selective colorization, and working with metadata. This chapter explains some of the tools available to obtain these results. Note that I will cover the most commonly used tools for retouching small portions of a photograph, but I'm not going into details about the techniques that some artists use for completely changing a photograph by painting on top of it.

Red-Eye Removal

Imagine yourself at a party. It is dark and a group of friends ask you to take a picture of them. You grab your camera, point, and shoot. The camera automatically turns on the flash as there is not enough ambient light available to produce a correct exposure. The result: half of your friends appear in the picture with two bright red circles instead of their eyes. This is a common problem in photography and it is called the *red-eye effect*.

The red-eye effect is caused because the light from the flash penetrates the eyes through the pupils, and then gets reflected to the camera from the back of the eyes where a large amount of blood is present. This blood is the reason why the eyes look red in the photograph. This effect is more noticeable when there is not much light in the environment and the pupils are dilated because of the dark. This is because pupils dilate when it is dark, allowing more light to get inside the eye and therefore producing a larger red-eye effect.

Once the photograph is taken, you can remove the red-eye effect easily by using image postprocessing. Figure 6-1 shows a before-and-after look at red-eye removal.

Figure 6-1. The right image shows the result of removing the red eyes from the original on the left side. The red-eye problem is solved, yet Gimp will preserve other red in the image.

Gimp offers an easy-to-use tool for removing the red-eye effect. First, you need to zoom in your image so that only the eyes appear on the screen, as Figure 6-2 shows. You can zoom in with several methods; using the plus (+) key on your keyboard, holding the Ctrl key and rotating your mouse wheel up, using the Zoom tool in the Toolbox, or even selecting View → Zoom and then choosing the zoom level that you need.

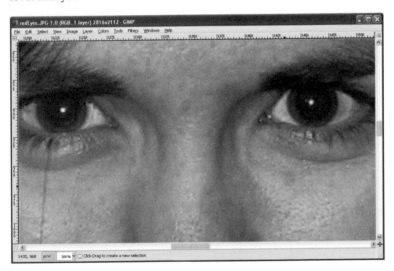

Figure 6-2. The red-eye effect portion of the image zoomed in

Then, you need to select both pupils in the image, which in this case are the areas that contain the red portion of the eyes. To do that, we are going to use the Ellipse Select tool, since the eyes are elliptical. In the Toolbox window, select the Ellipse Select tool, as shown in Figure 6-3.

Figure 6-3. The Ellipse Select tool in the Toolbox

Now we need to select one of the eyes. Click and drag your mouse around one eye; try to cover the entire red area. Don't worry if your selection wasn't perfect at the first try, you can alter the selection by dragging its sides.

The next step is to select the other eye as well. You need to tell Gimp that you want to add another area to the selection you currently have. Do this by holding the Shift key in your keyboard (use the Ctrl key to remove areas). Note how a plus sign (+) is added to the cursor when the key is pressed. While holding the Shift key, repeat the selection process for the other eye. After finishing the selection and then releasing the Shift key, you can adjust the new selection by dragging its sides.

Now select Filters → Enhance → Red Eye Removal. The Red Eye Removal dialog box shown in Figure 6-4 will appear.

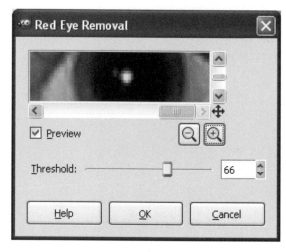

Figure 6-4. Gimp's Red Eye Removal dialog box, with a correct Threshold setting

Once you are inside the Red Eye Removal dialog box, you can preview how the effect will look. You can zoom in or out and move the location of the preview window. The Threshold parameter allows you to increase or decrease the level of redness to remove. If you select a threshold that is too low, red areas will remain in the eye. If you select a threshold that is too high, the effect may look unrealistic.

After selecting the correct Threshold and clicking OK in the Red Eye Removal dialog box, you can see how your image is now free from the red-eye effect.

Object Removal

In some situations, you may have the need to remove unwanted objects in photos. These objects can actually be anything, such as little imperfections on the skin of a person, leaves, stones, animals, people, and many other possibilities.

The technique used to remove objects is to generate a texture from the surroundings of the object to be removed and then cover the object's area with the generated texture. By doing that, the object is removed from the scene. Figures 6-5 and 6-6 show a more extreme example. Note that you normally would not remove the main subject of a photograph. I did it in this example to show you how versatile this tool is; although the removed object was fairly large, the texture used to fill in where the bird was is nearly impossible to detect.

Figure 6-5. This image shows the original photograph of a bird on a cluttered background

Figure 6-6. This image shows the previous photograph processed. Note how the bird disappeared.

Removing Objects with Gimp

Gimp offers many tools for removing unwanted objects in your photographs. One of the most powerful and easy-to-use is Resynthesizer, which is a Gimp plug-in. It is an excellent piece of software made by Paul Harrison as part of his PhD. You can get instructions on how to download and install it from this book's Appendix.

The first step is to roughly select the object that you want to remove. You can use the Free Select tool, which looks like a lasso, from the Toolbox window (see Figure 6-7) to freely select the contour of the object. You don't need to be precise, just make a quick selection that contains the object that you want to remove. Make your first click near the boundary of the object, then proceed clicking around the boundary until you finally click on the original point a second time. Figure 6-8 shows what this looks like when you're done. You can get more information about selecting a region in Chapter 5.

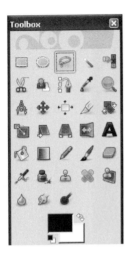

Figure 6-7. The Free Select tool from the Toolbox window in Gimp

Figure 6-8. This image shows the object selected loosely using the Free Select tool. You may have to look closely to see the dashed outline because of the texture in the grass.

Then, you need to select Filters → Enhance → Heal Selection, which opens the dialog box shown in Figure 6-9. Remember that you have to first install the plug-in to have this option enabled in Gimp.

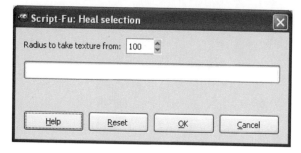

Figure 6-9. Gimp's Heal Selection dialog box

To generate the texture, the program searches for repeated patterns in the surroundings of the area you selected, so that the newly generated patch will seamlessly blend with its surroundings. The only parameter that you need to define is the radius where the program will search. This is measured from around the area that you have selected. The larger this value is, the greater the area around the selection for finding a good texture will be. Try using low numbers first (100 or less) and see if you can get good results. If it does not produce the result you were expecting, try increasing this radius until you get good results. Remember that you may not want to increase this radius too much because different areas of the image may get copied into the selection. For example, if you are removing a person from the sand on a beach, you want to cover him only with sand, but if you increase the radius too much, you could end up covering him with parts of the sea or the sky.

The size of the objects than you can remove is not necessarily small, as you could see in the previous image. It was an example of a large object, an entire bird, being removed completely from a cluttered background. Next, I will show you how to remove multiple small objects from a scene, as shown in Figures 6-10 and 6-11.

Figure 6-10. *This image shows an Australian White Ibis. Note how the right side of the image shows a lot of distracting elements such as another bird, the rocks on the path, the grass, and the leaf at the top.*

Figure 6-11. *This image shows the previous image processed. Many objects were removed from the right side.*

The first thing to do is to remove the leaves from the upper right corner. As these objects are isolated and only surrounded by water, it will be an easy fix. As always, you need to select the objects that you want to remove. In this case, you'd select both leaves using the Free Select tool. Remember that you can add another object to the selection by holding the Shift key in your keyboard while you select the other object. It does not matter much if you select some water; just make sure that the entire object is inside your selection, as Figure 6-12 shows.

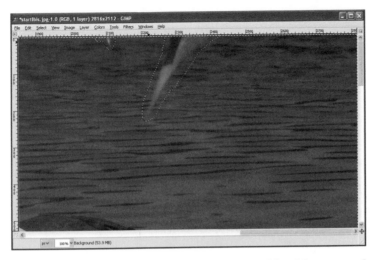

Figure 6-12. This image shows both leaves selected for object removal with Gimp.

Once both leaves are selected, just remove them by using the previously explained plug-in, as shown in Figure 6-13. This shows you that you can use this plug-in to remove large or small objects.

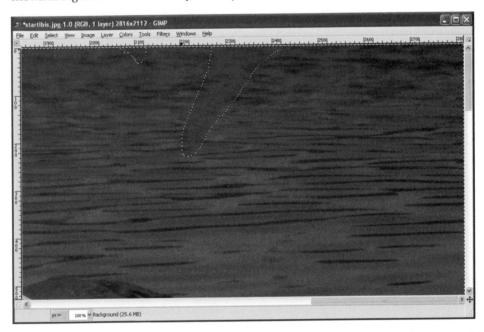

Figure 6-13. This image shows how both leaves disappeared after processing the image with the default value for the radius.

Removing Objects with the Clone Tool

Let's remove the other bird that you can see behind the White Ibis. This case is a little more complex than the leaves because the object is not isolated. For this task, I will use the Clone tool. This tool allows you to copy regions from other parts of the image. You can access this tool by pressing C in your keyboard, or by selecting it from the Toolbox window as shown in Figure 6-14.

Figure 6-14. Selecting the Clone tool in Gimp

After you select the Clone tool, you first need to set the area from which you want to copy the pixels. Do this by just moving the mouse there, holding the Ctrl key, and clicking your mouse. Now you are ready to paint over the object. For this example, I set the water as the cloning region, as shown in Figure 6-15. Note that you can choose any brush size or shape in the Clone Options window (under the Toolbox). Changing the brush properties changes the way you paint. Larger brushes produce larger effects, while its shape determines how it is painted. I recommend that you use the largest circular brush that fits in the object that you want to remove. This is because you will paint it faster and the borders will be smoother.

Figure 6-15. The Clone tool, ready to start painting over the object. Note that the circle with the cross is the region that is going to be copied into the other circle when clicked, removing the bird manually.

Once you click your mouse, the contents of the cloning region are copied to where your mouse is. If you maintain the button pressed and move the mouse, the cloning region will move as well, copying the corresponding areas, as shown in Figure 6-16. Once you release the button, the cloning region goes back to its original position. You can reset the cloning region any time you want by just pressing Ctrl and clicking on the new region. You may notice that when cloning large regions of the image, the result is not very realistic. For solving this, you can change the clone source to different but roughly similar areas, mixing them to avoid repeating and banding.

Figure 6-16. This image shows the result of cloning the water nearby to remove the bird.

As you can see in Figure 6-16, the result of removing the other bird is not bad at all, although some borders are too evident. For solving that, you can use the Smudge tool. You can use it to blend the borders of the removed object. You can access the Smudge tool by either pressing the S key or selecting it from the Toolbox, as shown in Figure 6-17.

Figure 6-17. Selecting the Smudge tool in Gimp

The Smudge tool mixes and blends color. You need to click on the color and then drag the mouse to where you want to move it. Think of it like putting your finger on a wet painting; you will move and merge the colors into the direction you move your finger. In this case, I used the Smudge tool to blend the details of the water for the removed object. As you can see in Figure 6-16, the borders of the circular brush are visible. On every part that it looked like an abrupt change, I just clicked and dragged the mouse using the Smudge tool. See the result in Figure 6-18.

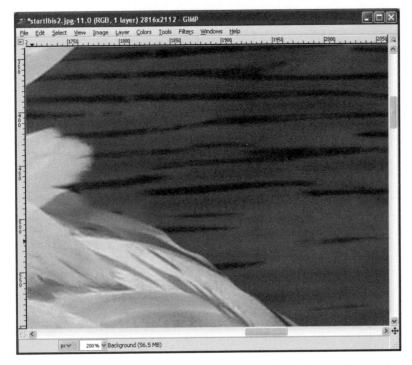

Figure 6-18. The Smudge tool can help you to diminish abrupt changes in your photographs.

Removing Small Objects with the Healing Tool

For removing the small objects, you can use the Healing Tool. This tool is similar to the Clone tool, except that the Healing tool blends the copied area with its surroundings. You can access the Healing tool by either pressing the H key or selecting it from the Toolbox, as shown in Figure 6-19.

Figure 6-19. *Accessing the Healing tool*

Select the brush size as the smallest circle that covers the object you want to remove, and then select a cloning region. Set it by holding the Ctrl key and clicking the mouse. I recommend that you choose an area adjacent to the item you want to remove, so that you obtain more natural looking images. Now just go to where the object is and click. It will be gone, merged with the background, as shown in Figure 6-20.

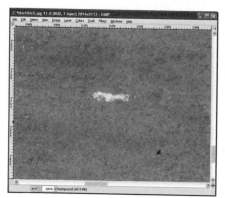
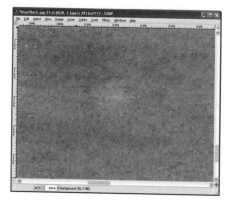

Figure 6-20. *This image shows the effect of the Healing tool for removing two objects, the big white mark in the middle and the small stone in the bottom right.*

As you can see, the Resynthesizer plug-in gives you the ability to remove all sorts of objects, large or small. You only need to roughly select the object that you want to remove and then apply the plug-in with the desired radius and it will take care of the rest. On the other hand, for more manual control, Gimp also gives you different tools such as the Clone and Healing tools, as well as the Smudge Tool.

Selective Colorization

The selective colorization technique has been very popular, as it can produce very pleasant results. It uses color foreground objects over a grayscale background to highlight specific objects. Figure 6-21 shows the image we will work with; we're going to have colored ducks on a grayscale background.

Figure 6-21. This is the original image.

For this effect you will need to use layers. You can think of layers as a set of transparencies. If you have two or more transparencies, you can put one on top of the other so that their contents get mixed into just one global visual representation. You can change each transparency individually and the result will be shown in the global visual representation. The same is true for layers. For example, you can have a background layer and a foreground layer. In the background layer, there may be a very dense jungle photograph. In the foreground layer, you may have a photograph of an isolated lion. By having these two images in different layers, you are able to easily move the lion into any position in the jungle. It does not matter if the background is very complex; in this case, foreground and background are independent because they are in separate layers.

Another concept that is going to be useful in this section is *masking*. A mask allows you to only use certain parts of a layer. You can think of a mask as a set of holes in a layer so that you can see through these holes to the lower layers.

Gimp offers Dockable Dialogs, which are many extra windows that you can enable or disable at any given time. These windows provide more information about your image. Some of these are the Image Channels, the Histogram, Image Layers, and many more. For this section, you will need the Layers window, which is devoted solely to the purpose of managing your photograph's layers and masks. You can open it by going to Windows → Dockable Dialogs → Layers. You can also open it quicker by just pressing Ctrl-L.

The Layers dialog box allows you to see all the layers and masks currently active in the image. Layers that are first on the list appear on top of the ones that appear below them. For now, there is only one layer named Background, as shown in Figure 6-22.

Figure 6-22. The Layers dialog box in Gimp

For achieving this effect, I will use two layers; one with full color and another one on top of it in grayscale. Then, I will add a mask to the grayscale layer (create holes in it) so that the colored ducks of the lower layer are visible.

The first step is to generate a copy of the active layer. To do that, you need to go to Layer → Duplicate Layer. An easier way to manage layers is by using the icons of the layers window. The first icon allows you to create a new layer, the next two icons allows you to move the current layer one level above or below. The fourth icon is the duplicate layer icon, which is the one you may use in this case. The fifth button allows you to anchor any floating selection in the layer, such as text, for example. The last icon removes the current layer from the image.

After duplicating the Background layer, you can see how a new layer appeared in the Layers dialog box. This new layer is named Background copy. Make sure that you have this copy selected by clicking on its name. The active layer is the one that appears in blue, as shown in Figure 6-23. This is very important because any changes that you make in the main image will be applied to the active layer only.

Figure 6-23. This image shows the duplicated layer in the Layers dialog box.

The next step is to convert the Background copy layer into grayscale. As you already know from Chapter 4, you can achieve this by selecting Colors → Desaturate.

Now, you need to create a mask. Go to Layer → Mask → Add Layer Mask. Make sure that the mask initialization selected is White (Full Opacity), and then click on the Add button. This will add a small white rectangle on the currently selected layer in the Layers dialog box, as Figure 6-24 shows. In a mask, grayscale is used to represent where the holes of the layer are. White means solid, or no holes, while black means transparent, or that there is a hole in there. Grayscale values in between mean that there is certain opacity of the layer in those points. For this example, I started with a completely white mask. This means that the active layer does not contain any holes at all. As you can see, there are many other options to initialize the values of the mask, which are all basically grayscale images to be copied into the mask. All you need to know is that white is solid and black is transparent (and everything in between). We added this mask so that we can then cut the holes for the colored ducks to appear from the layer below.

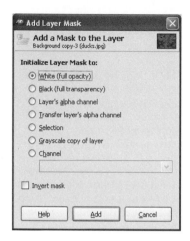 

Figure 6-24. The left image shows the Add Layer Mask dialog box and the right image shows it added to the current layer.

The next step is to select the objects that you want to appear as colorized, as shown in Figure 6-25. Select as many objects as you like using any of the selection tools available. You can read more about selection tools in Chapter 5. For example, you may use the Select by Color tool if you want to highlight objects of a specific color. In my case, I used the Free Selection tool.

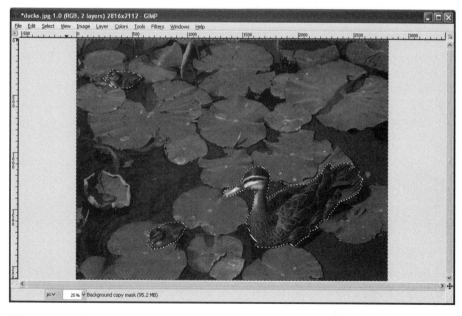

Figure 6-25. This image shows the objects to be colorized selected using the Free Selection tool.

After selecting the objects, you may want to smooth the borders of the selection. You can do that by choosing Selection → Feather. After that, a dialog box will appear, asking how many pixels you want to feather the selection. The more pixels you use, the larger the smooth border will be. Values between 5 and 10 pixels usually give good results.

Now, the only thing left to do is to cut the holes in the current layer. This is done by painting black over the mask in the regions that I just selected. Make sure that the mask is selected in the Layers window. Click in the white rectangle next to the current layer to select it. You can toggle from painting the mask to painting the layer by clicking on the one you want to edit in the Layers window. The rectangle on the left represents the layer, while the rectangle in the right represents the mask.

Once you have selected the mask, make sure that you have black selected as your foreground color and go to Edit → Fill with FG Color. This will paint the selected regions with black. This means that those regions will be transparent and therefore you can see the colored ducks from the layer below. Note that you can manually paint the mask using any type of brush that you want. I used the Fill with FG Color because it was easier for me; just one click. If selecting the region you want to paint is complicated, such as a region with holes in it for example, it may be easier to use the Paint Brush tool to paint it. In either case, what you want to paint is a mask similar to the one shown in Figure 6-26.

Figure 6-26. This image shows the mask applied to the top (grayscale) layer. Note how the holes (black areas) are exactly where the ducks are, allowing the bottom (color) layer to show the colored ducks only.

I have just scratched the surface here with layers and masks, but the basics are there and now you can use multiple layers when editing your images as well as adding masks to them for creating different effects such as selective colorization. Now I will introduce you to a different topic; metadata, or information about your photographs.

Metadata

Exchangeable image file format (EXIF) is a standard that provides information about images. A digital camera can provide very detailed information, including the date, owner, model, aperture, shutter speed, ISO a thumbnail, and many other values specific to the shot made (in some models, even the camera temperature). Image editing programs can read or modify these values as well. You can see a subset of this information without any special software on Windows XP and Ubuntu.

On Windows XP, right-click on any image, select Properties, go to the Summary tab, and finally click on Advanced to see the metadata of the image, shown in Figure 6-27.

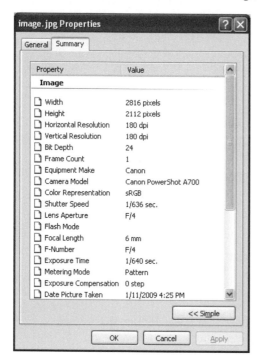

Figure 6-27. A subset of a photograph metadata is presented in Windows XP, without any additional software.

On Ubuntu, right-click on any image, select Properties, then go to the Image tab to see the metadata of the image, as shown in Figure 6-28.

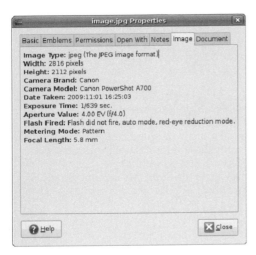

Figure 6-28. A subset of a photograph metadata is presented in Ubuntu, without any additional software.

ExifTool

The most complete tool for working with metadata is ExifTool. You can use it to read, write, and modify metadata from photographs, music, and even video files. ExifTool works in the command line and accepts many arguments. You can mix different arguments for achieving the desired result. If you haven't done so, please check the Appendix for instructions on how to install ExifTool.

Next, I'll go over some functionalities of ExifTool.

Reading Metadata

For reading all the information about a photograph named Image.jpg, just go to the command line, change your directory to the one where the image is, and type the following:

```
exiftool Image.jpg
```

If you want to store the output of the program in a text file, you only need to add the -w .txt argument to the program, which means that you want to write the output in a file with the .txt extension and with the same name of the photograph. This is very handy for accessing the information later, as shown in Figure 6-29. The syntax for this command is as follows:

```
exiftool -w .txt Image.jpg
```

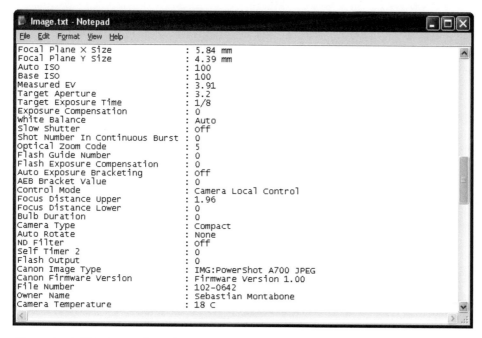

```
Image.txt - Notepad
File  Edit  Format  View  Help
Focal Plane X Size              : 5.84 mm
Focal Plane Y Size              : 4.39 mm
Auto ISO                        : 100
Base ISO                        : 100
Measured EV                     : 3.91
Target Aperture                 : 3.2
Target Exposure Time            : 1/8
Exposure Compensation           : 0
White Balance                   : Auto
Slow Shutter                    : Off
Shot Number In Continuous Burst : 0
Optical Zoom Code               : 5
Flash Guide Number              : 0
Flash Exposure Compensation     : 0
Auto Exposure Bracketing        : Off
AEB Bracket Value               : 0
Control Mode                    : Camera Local Control
Focus Distance Upper            : 1.96
Focus Distance Lower            : 0
Bulb Duration                   : 0
Camera Type                     : Compact
Auto Rotate                     : None
ND Filter                       : Off
Self Timer 2                    : 0
Flash Output                    : 0
Canon Image Type                : IMG:PowerShot A700 JPEG
Canon Firmware Version          : Firmware Version 1.00
File Number                     : 102-0642
Owner Name                      : Sebastian Montabone
Camera Temperature              : 18 C
```

Figure 6-29. This image shows how detailed the metadata can be when extracted with ExifTool.

You can filter the list to only show specific properties of interest. For example, if you want to see only the size of the image and its exposure time, you can execute this:

```
exiftool -ImageSize -ExposureTime Image.jpg
```

You can see the list of all the possible properties that the program can access for a given photograph in the left column of the output of the following command (see Figure 6-30):

```
exiftool -s Image.jpg
```

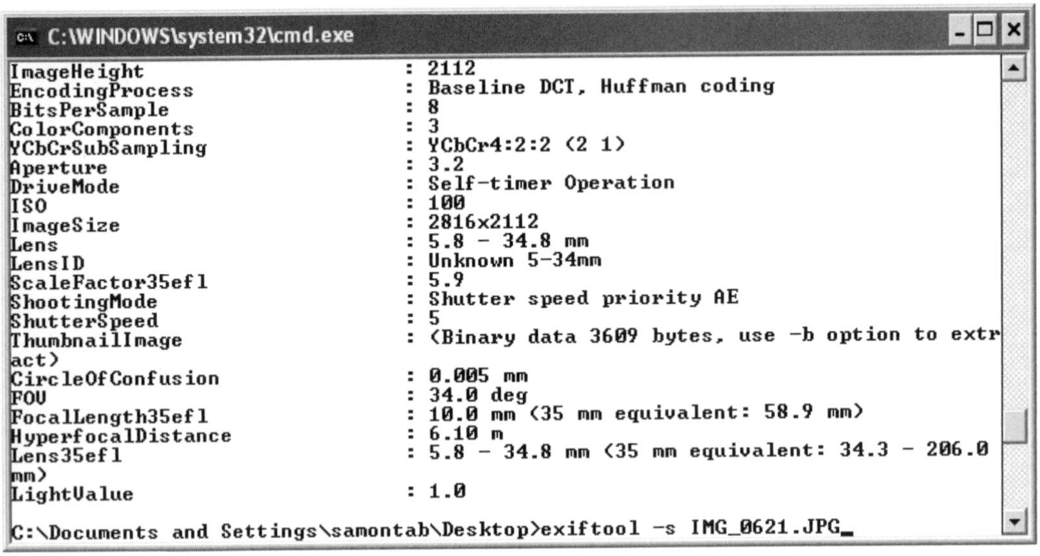

Figure 6-30. *Available metadata properties in ExifTool*

You can get a text file output just by mixing both options. Using the following command, you can create customized text files showing only the properties you need (see Figure 6-31):

```
exiftool -w .txt -ShutterSpeedValue -ApertureValue -ISO -DateTimeOriginal Image.jpg
```

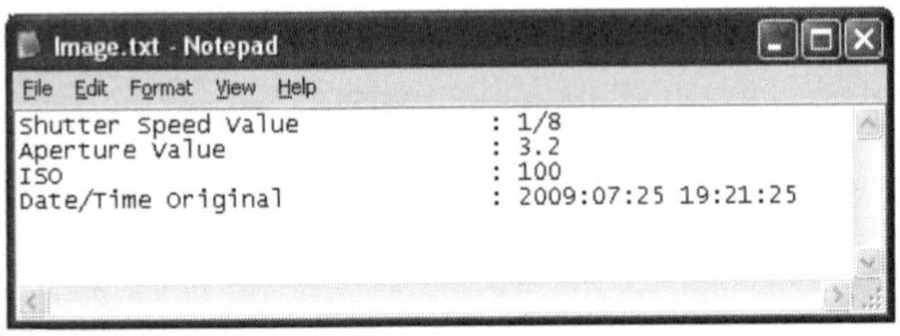

Figure 6-31. *A customized text file created with the metadata of a photograph*

If instead of a text file, you would like to generate a table for a web page, you just need to add the -h option and change the filetype, as follows:

```
exiftool -h -w .htm -ShutterSpeedValue -ApertureValue -ISO -DateTimeOriginal Image.jpg
```

Now that we know how to read metadata from one image, the next step is to read it from many images. The first step is to put all your images inside one folder and give that folder name as the argument to the program. In this example, the folder will be called pictures. Move that folder onto your desktop. Now, open the command line and write the following:

```
cd Desktop
exiftool -w .txt -r pictures
```

Figure 6-32 shows the results.

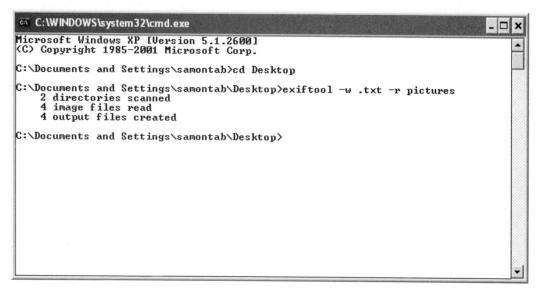

Figure 6-32. An example of how to write text files with metadata for any number of files

The -r option is to make the program recursive, which means that it will search for pictures that are in folders inside the folder you specified. Putting everything together, you can make your own custom metadata text files for all your photo collections. Here is one example for doing just that:

```
exiftool -w .txt -r -ShutterSpeedValue -ApertureValue -ISO -DateTimeOriginal pictures
```

Note that the program will not overwrite text files, so if you've already created a text file for an image, it will skip it. You can just erase the text files if you want the program to regenerate them.

Some images also contain embedded thumbnails or preview images. In general, thumbnails are just small versions of the main image, but sometimes thumbnails are not updated along with the main image and therefore show a preview of an older version of the image. If the thumbnail is different than the main image, it may be due to copyright infringement; someone may have cropped or removed the copyright text in the main image, for example, and the thumbnail was not updated. You can extract the thumbnail embedded in an image using the following code:

```
exiftool -b -ThumbnailImage Image.jpg > Thumbnail.jpg
```

Modifying Metadata

In some cases, metadata of an image may no longer be available or accurate after editing it. In these cases, you may want to copy the metadata from one file to another. You can execute the following code to achieve that:

```
exiftool -tagsfromfile [SourceImage] [DestinationImage]
```

For example, if you have an original photograph called original.jpg and, after making some changes to it, you obtained an image called processed.jpg that has lost its metadata, you can copy it back from the original with this code:

```
exiftool -tagsfromfile original.jpg processed.jpg
```

In other cases, you may want to erase all the metadata from a file. You can achieve that by running the following command (note that there is a space between the equal sign and the image file name):

```
exiftool -all= Image.jpg
```

To change the embedded thumbnail image, you need a separate image that will be embedded into the main image. Usually to create a thumbnail, the main image is reduced to about 160x120 pixels. To embed the image Thumbnail.jpg into Image.jpg, you can execute the following code:

```
exiftool "-ThumbnailImage<=Thumbnail.jpg" Image.jpg
```

Organizing Files Using Metadata

Some users might consider this section to be advanced. It is not strictly necessary for processing your images, but managing hundreds or thousands of images based on file name alone is impossible. To find a photo, taken years ago, buried on your hard drive, is nearly impossible unless you can search using some sort of metadata (information and keywords) about the image. Without metadata, your only search tools are folder name, file name, and waiting for thumbnails to be displayed. With good metadata, you can narrow your search very quickly.

ExifTool also allows you to organize your files based on their metadata. For example, if you have all your images in one folder, you can organize them by the dates they were taken, so you would have a folder for each year, month, and day with the corresponding pictures inside. This hierarchy can be based on anything the program can read (exposure time, ISO, and so forth), but date is the one of the most common properties for arranging photographs. Make sure you back up your data before executing the following codes, as you will be moving and renaming your files.

You can organize your photos in the previously described hierarchy with this code:

```
exiftool "-Directory<DateTimeOriginal" -d %Y/%m/%d *
```

The asterisk means that we are going to process all the files. The -d option gives the date format, which in this case is Year/Month/Day. DateTimeOriginal is the date when the photograph was taken, and the Directory keyword means that we are giving the directory where we want to move the pictures.

If you already have a hierarchy of directories and want to have all your pictures in just one folder, you can also do this with ExifTool. The following code will move all the files found recursively in the folder hierarchy into the current directory. Note that there are two dots separated by a space at the end.

```
exiftool -r -Directory=. .
```

You can also change the file names of your images using ExifTool. You do this with the filename keyword. Special variables that you can use are %f, which is the original filename; %e, which is the extension of the image (such as JPG); and %d, which is the directory of the file. Also, you can access all the properties that the program can read. You only need to enclose the property name with ${}. For example, you can append the aperture and the ISO to the images file name and precede the file name with the make of the camera with this code:

```
exiftool "-filename<${Make}_%f_${ApertureValue}_${ISO}.%e" .
```

The image IMG_0655.JPG would be renamed to Canon_IMG_0655_3.5_100.JPG, where the aperture value is 3.5, the ISO setting is 100, the make is Canon, and the original file name is maintained in between these values. This renaming scheme is very powerful and flexible and allows you to specify any format you desire. You can add the -r option to make the command recursive (rename all the images that are inside folders of the current folder).

Take precaution with properties that their values may contain slashes (/), such as exposure time, because a slash in the filename can be interpreted as a path and you will end up creating a directory instead of just renaming the file.

Using a combination of the previous examples, you can organize your own digital photo collection based on metadata. This can be very useful for archiving and accessing digital photos. For further research, consider researching Digital Asset Management (DAM) systems, or using image organizers such as digiKam.

Summary

In this chapter, you have learned how to retouch your photos. You can now fix red eyes in your images, and remove unwanted objects of any size automatically. Also, you can remove small objects manually. You also know how to work with layers and masks for making fine adjustments such as selective colorization. Another thing that you can do now is to work with metadata. You can read and write metadata in an image, and you can even organize your photos automatically with it.

In the next chapter, you will learn how to create HDR photographs from ordinary images.

■ ■ ■

HDR Imaging

Picture this: You are staring at an incredible landscape. The view is amazing, the sky is clear, and the sun is shining, producing a rich mixture of highlights and shadows. You take as many pictures as you can and then start your trip back after contemplating the landscape once again. After you arrive home and look at your pictures on the computer, you realize that the images do not give justice to what you just saw. It seems to you that the camera, somehow, was not able to capture the richness of the landscape. In some pictures, you have a nice exposure of the darker areas of the landscape, while the bright areas, where the sun was being reflected, look almost white without showing any details. On other pictures, you got a nice exposure of those bright areas, but in those pictures, the darker areas look too black to see the details on them properly.

This lack of details in the highlights or shadows in the images is because digital cameras in general have a low *dynamic range*. This means that, in a single shot, the difference between the brightest bright and the darkest dark that the camera can capture is small. The difference in brightness that you and I are capable of perceiving, in a given lighting condition, is many times larger than the one that a camera is able to capture in a single shot. Take for instance a regular digital camera that generates JPG images, which is a common case. The final image that this particular camera produces has only 256 distinct levels of light, while the human eye can perceive more than 10,000 levels of light in a given lighting condition. This means that you need to choose wisely how to use that limited dynamic range by changing the controls of the camera to accommodate the light present in the scene. However, in a contrasting scene, where some areas are very bright and others very dark, you can only capture the highlights or the shadows, but you cannot capture both in the same shot because of the low dynamic range that most digital cameras have. If the camera is set to capture the highlights, darker parts of the image will look entirely black. On the other hand, if you set the camera to capture the shadows, brighter parts of the image will look completely white. In photographic terms, those areas would be under- and overexposed, respectively. There is no setting in your camera that will allow you to get that shot right.

Here is where *HDR Imaging* comes in handy. HDR stands for High Dynamic Range. These images use a large number of bits per channel to represent an image, giving them the ability to differentiate the same or even more levels of light than the human eye is capable of. This means that HDR images are able to store much more details about highlights and shadows than regular, or Low Dynamic Range (LDR) images and therefore are able to represent both highlights and shadows in the same image. Figures 7-1 and 7-2 show the difference between LDR and HDR.

The general workflow for these types of images is to first generate an HDR image and then tone-map it to an LDR image so that you can save it in a more standard format while preserving the most important details of the HDR image. I will show you now how to achieve these two steps.

Figure 7-1. *This is the photograph that the camera produces with its automatic exposure settings. Note how the camera is not able to reproduce the highlights or the shadows in the same image.*

Figure 7-2. *This image shows the final photograph after the HDR imaging procedures have been applied. Note how detail is present in highlights and shadows. This photograph is much more similar to what a human observer would have seen in the scene than the previous image.*

Generating an HDR Image

The main difference between an HDR and an LDR image is their color depth. Usually, images with a color depth of 8 bits or less per channel are called LDR images. They are very common, JPG images being one example, and widely supported in many image editing programs. On the other hand, images with a color depth of more than 8 bits per channel are usually called HDR images. They are less common and also less supported. Some examples of HDR images are RAW images, 16-bit TIFF (.tif), OpenEXR (.exr), and Radiance (.hdr), among others.

RAW files can generate HDR images because they normally use 10 or more bits for color depth. Keep in mind though that only one RAW image may not be enough to cover the dynamic range of a scene. If the RAW image has a color depth of 10 bits, it means that it can represent up to 4 times the dynamic range a JPG image can, whereas humans can differentiate up to 40 times the dynamic range of a JPG image.

You have two options for creating an HDR image; you can generate it with just one RAW file or you can take multiple shots of the scene and then merge them. I will show you both methods.

Generating an HDR Image from One RAW File

The RAW file format actually is just the information that comes directly from the sensor. At this point, it is just a set of values that represent how much light was sensed at different places of the sensor. It does not represent an image the same as the other formats. RAW is like the negative in film photography; you need to process it in order to obtain a color image. When the digital camera saves a digital image (a .jpg file for instance), it means that the processing was done inside the camera. This is the easiest and most common case, although higher-end cameras offer an option for saving raw data that gives more control to the photographer. Using the raw data, the photographer can adjust the parameters needed to create a digital image later using software in a PC instead of letting the camera guess all the parameters when the picture is taken.

As we already know, light can be decomposed into three components: red, green, and blue. We can generate any specific color by mixing different intensities of those three lights. The same is true if you want to sense color instead of generate it. If you try to pass light through a blue filter, for instance, only the blue component of light can pass and you can measure its intensity. That way, using three different filters—one for red, one for green and one for blue—you can measure the intensity of the incoming light for each component. With those three values, you have the color of the incoming light.

Inside most of today's digital cameras, to reduce the cost of putting three separate filters, light passes through a single color filter mosaic. On every one of the pixels of the filter, only the red, blue, or green component of the incoming light passes and gets sensed and stored, among other values, as the raw data. One of the most commonly used color filter mosaics is the Bayer pattern. It is a 2x2 pattern that has one red, one blue, and two green filters. There are more green filters because humans are more sensitive to green light.

The process of converting the information from the color filter mosaic into separate color channels is called *demosaicing*. These three separate color channels, usually in the RGB color space, are needed to create the digital image, as Figure 7-3 shows.

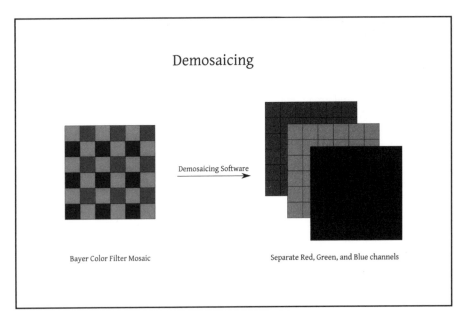

Figure 7-3. This diagram shows the process of demosaicing.

Demosaicing with UFRaw

UFRaw is very useful software that lets you develop your RAW images into a more standard format and provides many options, as shown in Figure 7-4. You can also use it as a plug-in for Gimp, allowing you to open RAW files with it. If you haven't done so, go to the Appendix for instructions on how to install it.

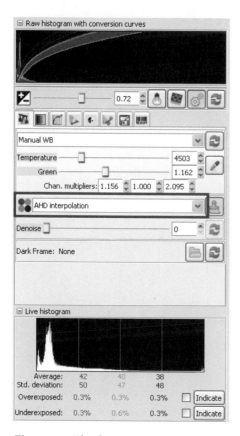

Figure 7-4. The demosaicing section of the UFRaw software.

The demosaicing algorithms implemented in UFRaw are Adaptive Homogeneity-Directed (AHD) interpolation, Variable Number of Gradients (VNG) interpolation, VNG four color, Patterned Pixel Grouping (PPG) interpolation, and Bilinear interpolation. Each of them produces slightly different results. I recommend that you use the AHD interpolation, which is one of the best algorithms available.

The correct white balance preset should be used in the camera when shooting JPG images. Raw data, on the other hand, is not tied to any particular white balance, so it can be easily set later in your digital darkroom. You can still try to adjust an incorrect white balance in digital images (as seen in Chapter 4), although you will get worse results than selecting the correct white balance in the camera or shooting with raw data. Fortunately, there are freely available tools for each situation.

Adjusting White Balance with UFRaw

If you have raw data, you can use UFRaw. With it, you can easily change the color temperature and the green channel intensity (see Figure 7-5).

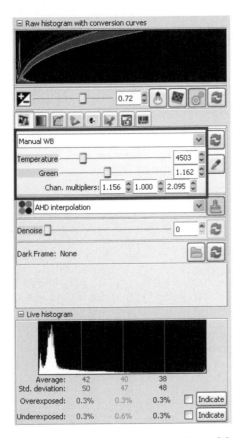

Figure 7-5. The white balance section of the UFRaw software

UFRaw allows you to select different presets for white balance, such as Daylight, Cloudy, Tungsten, and Flash. You only need to select the specific preset according to the source light and the colors are automatically corrected for you. Also, you can select Auto White Balance (WB), which automatically corrects the image colors for you. Auto WB works reasonably well in most situations. If you need more control or you want to create artistic effects, you can always use the Manual WB. This mode allows you to specify the exact color temperature and green channel intensity of the scene. For example, if you select a low temperature, it means that you are telling UFRaw that the source light was reddish. UFRaw will then try to remove the reddish cast on the image by increasing the color temperature of the image. Also, there is an eyedropper that allows you to click on a white, gray, or black point in the image to use it as the reference. First, you have to click on the point in the image and then you have to click on the eyedropper. UFRaw will use that point as the reference and calculate all the white balance parameters automatically.

The histogram in the bottom part of the screen shows you how each color is distributed in the image. If you have an image with low values of a specific color, you will see a curve of that particular color with a peak on the left side of the histogram. If the image is very bright in that specific color, you will see a peak on the right side. In this case, because the image is dark, all three channels in the histogram appear with a peak on the left side, which means that they have low values. You can see that there are three curves, one for red, one for green, and one for Blue. When two or more curves are on top of each other, they are presented as if they are merged using additive color mixing (remember Chapter 2?). That is why most of the curve in this case is shown as white, since the three channels are on top of each other.

Once you are happy with the colors of your image, you can save it in any HDR format. You can now go to the "Tone Mapping" section later in this chapter for the next steps.

Generating an HDR Image from Multiple Pictures

The main idea for generating this type of HDR images is to take multiple pictures of exactly the same scene, with each LDR picture representing a "slice" of the possible HDR; some pictures will have the details of the brightest parts, and others will have the details of the darkest parts. In theory, you can do this can by changing any of the controls of the camera, but it is recommended that you only change the exposure time, not aperture or ISO. This is because changing the aperture changes which objects are in focus in the images, but you want them all to keep the same focus in all the pictures. By changing the ISO, the result is that some images may have considerably more noise than others, making it more difficult to achieve natural-looking stitched images. On the other hand, if you change the exposure time, and none of your subjects are moving, the changes in the images will almost only be the details in shadows or highlights, which is exactly what you are looking for. It is very important to keep the camera as still as possible so that the resulting images cover exactly the same scene. Some cameras support a mode called *bracketing* that allows you to take multiple shots while automatically changing the exposure settings. Check your camera manual if it has this option available. If your camera does not support exposure bracketing, you can still take every shot manually, although it will take you longer and the scene may have changed noticeably, such as a traffic scene. Also, you may have accidentally moved the camera while changing the settings.

To generate an HDR image with this method, you will need at least two images taken with different exposure settings, although five or more can give better results. You need to make sure that you cover the entire dynamic range of the scene with the images that you are taking; this means that you need to have at least one image where the brightest parts of the scene are well exposed and at least another image where the darkest parts of the scene are well exposed and free of noise. Also, you should have images in between. As a general rule of thumb, I suggest you to use three shots; one with a well-balanced exposition, one underexposed, and another one overexposed. In general, it is recommended to change the exposure by one or two stops on each step until you cover the entire dynamic range of the scene. Figures 7-6 through 7-8 show an example of this range.

■ **Note** In photography, a *stop* is a relative exposure value. Adding one full stop means that the total amount of light in the exposure is doubled, while decreasing one full stop means that it is halved. You can achieve this by changing any of the three exposure controls: exposure time, aperture, or ISO. Note that, for example, if you double the amount of light by increasing the exposure time and halve the amount of light by reducing the ISO, the exposure remains the same. In that case, you did not change any stops in the exposure and the image will have the same amount of light, but you will have the effects of the increased exposure time (moving objects will appear blurrier) and the decreased ISO (the image will present less noise). If you are learning how to get a proper exposure, you can always first get the exposure automatically from the camera. You can look at the proposed values of the three controls and then go to manual mode with those settings initially and start balancing the controls to achieve different effects while you maintain the exposure.

The set of images are then mixed together into a single image that has a large color depth and represents the full dynamic range of the scene. There are many ways to mix the images together. You need to set a weighting function, a response curve, and an HDR creation model. The weighting function is how the pixels of the different images are combined together. You could use a simple average, or you can apply any other function, such as a Gaussian function, for example. The response curve refers to the response of the camera to light. This curve relates the amount of light received with the actual values that are recorded in the camera. There are two main cases, when the response curve is linear and when it is Gamma (that is, non-linear). Raw data is captured linearly, which means that the numbers stored in the RAW format are a constant multiplied by the amount of light received. On the other hand, processed images, such as JPG files, have a nonlinear response curve. This means that if a pixel in a JPG file has twice the value of another one, it does not mean that there was the double amount of light in that particular position. Finally, the HDR creation model defines how the previous parameters are mixed together to generate the HDR.

Figure 7-6. This image shows a photograph taken by decreasing the exposure time by two full stops, allowing the brightest parts of the image to be properly exposed.

Figure 7-7. *This image shows the photograph taken with the automatic settings of the camera for reference.*

Figure 7-8. *Increasing the exposure time by two full stops reveals the details from the darkest parts of the scene.*

Generating the HDR Image with Qtpfsgui

The software that allows us to generate HDR images with multiple images is called Qtpfsgui. You may think that the authors of this software just selected random letters to create a very hard-to-pronounce name. The reality is that this name actually tells you a lot about the software. *Qt* is a cross-platform framework (and a very good one), so it tells you that this program uses that programming framework so that the software can run on any computer. This software is also based on the code of the projects PFStools, PFSmo, and PFScalibration, which all relate to HDR imaging. That's where the *pfs* part of the name comes from. And finally, *GUI* stands for Graphical User Interface, so you know that you will not need to go to the command line in order to use it. Although now the name of this software possibly makes a little more sense to you, Qtpfsgui will be renamed to a simpler name, Luminance HDR, from version 2.0 onwards. If you haven't done so, go to the Appendix to download and install it.

The usual workflow in Qtpfsgui is to first create or load an HDR image, then select the tone mapping operator to be used, and finally save the LDR image as a regular digital image. To create an HDR image, you need to click on the New HDR button on the toolbar, or go to the File menu and select the New HDR option. The dialog box shown in Figure 7-9 appears.

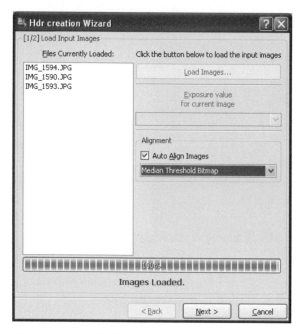

Figure 7-9. The dialog for creating a new HDR image in Qtpfsgui

The first thing that you must do is to load the images. Click on the Load Images button shown in Figure 7-9 and select all the images that you want to combine to make the HDR image. Remember that there should be at least two images. You can select multiple images by holding the Ctrl key on your keyboard while you select the file names, or by selecting a rectangular area covering the images that you want to select. Make sure that the Auto Align Images option is checked because if your images are not properly aligned, the final result will be blurry. You can either select hugin's align_image_stack or the Median Threshold Bitmap option. Both work relatively well, although the hugin's align_image_stack option may sometimes be slower. If you have problems with one, try the other. In the next window, you can manually adjust the images so that they are exactly in the same position, as Figure 7-10 shows. This is usually not necessary since the automatic alignment delivers good results.

CHAPTER 7 ■ HDR IMAGING

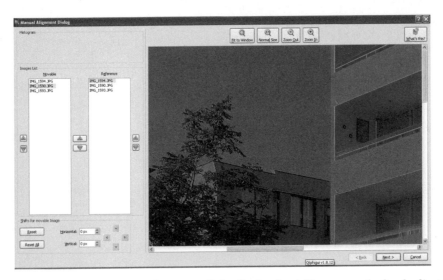

Figure 7-10. The manual alignment dialog for Qtpfsgui. You can make final adjustments here, but you can generally skip this dialog box since automatic alignment works well most of the time.

Now you can select which profile you want to use to generate the HDR image, as Figure 7-11 shows. Each profile selects different options for generating the HDR. There are three parameters that are indirectly selected by the profiles: Weighting function, Response Curve, and the HDR creation model. The default option, Profile 1, selects Triangular, Gamma, and Debevec respectively. Most users are happy with the results of Profile 1, so if you are not interested in the details of creating an HDR image, you can click on the Finish button now.

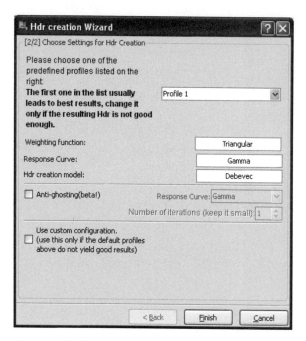

Figure 7-11. The dialog box for creating the HDR image

If you want to explore the details of HDR creation, you can change the selection to another profile or check the Use Custom Configuration option. This will allow you to manually select which weighting function, response curve, and HDR creation model to use for the HDR generation, as shown in Figure 7-12. A Triangular or Gaussian function is a good option for a weighting function. If you are using RAW images, you should choose a linear response curve, and if you are using processed images, such as .jpg files, you should select Gamma. In the HDR creation model there are two options, Debevec and Robertson. I recommend that you use the Debevec option, although both can give good results. After you select your options, click on the Finish button.

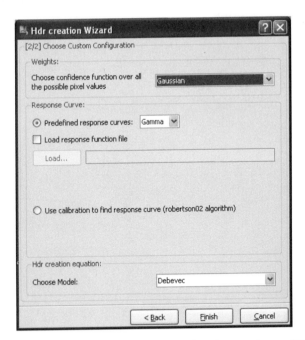

Figure 7-12. The advanced dialog box for creating an HDR image

After you click Finish, the HDR image is generated using the selected options. Once it is finished, a preview of it will appear on screen, as shown in Figure 7-13. What you are looking at is only a preview of the HDR using a simple linear mapping. You can change the mapping if you want; it is only for visualization purposes. You can save the HDR here so you can access it later. Do this by clicking the Save Hdr As button.

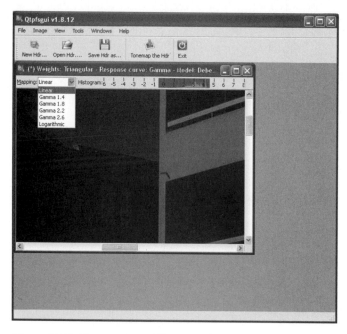

Figure 7-13. The preview of the recently created HDR image

Tone Mapping

One of the problems with HDR images is that most computer displays or printers only work with LDR images. This means that an HDR image needs to be converted into an LDR image in order to be seen on a computer display or printed. The process of converting an HDR image into an LDR image is called *tone mapping*.

There are many options to tone-map an existing HDR image. The simplest would be linearly reducing the contrast of the image. Although it solves the color depth problem, the results are similar to just taking one photograph in the first place: detail is lost. More advanced techniques use the available 8 bits per channel in a more intelligent way so that contrast and details of the original HDR image are preserved as much as possible in the LDR image. These techniques are commonly known as *tone mapping operators*.

I do not recommend using Gimp for HDR. This is because the core of Gimp uses only 8 bits per channel, which is useful only for LDR images. There are many so-called HDR images made with Gimp that are very basic or not HDR at all.

Tone Mapping with Qtpfsgui

At this point, you should have already created your HDR image. It does not matter if you used only a single RAW file or a set of multiple LDR images. In any case, you should have an HDR image open in Qtpfsgui. If you saved the HDR, you can open it now by clicking on the Open Hdr button or select File— Open Hdr. This will open the file selector dialog box. Select the HDR image that you want to tone-map and then click Open.

Now what you need to do is to click on the Tonemap the HDR button or select the Image menu and then choose the Tonemap the HDR option. This will open a new window that allows you to select which operator you will be using for tone mapping, the options specific to the selected operator, and some common options.

The first option that you should select is the size of the resulting image, shown in Figure 7-14. Selecting a small size first allows you to quickly preview the results of different operators and different parameters by clicking on the Apply button. You can then select a larger size and process it with the parameters you selected. It is recommended that you first use the default parameters and then start exploring while changing small values, one parameter at a time, as in Figure 7-15.

The Pre Tone mapping gamma adjustment slider affects all tone mapping operators. You can make nonlinear adjustments to the resulting image by changing this slider.

You can save any file at any time by selecting the image and clicking on the Save As button. Keep in mind that you need to set the resolution of the image before you process it. Also note that larger images will need longer processing times. You can always process small resolution first, change parameters, and see how they look in your image before you increase the resolution for the final image.

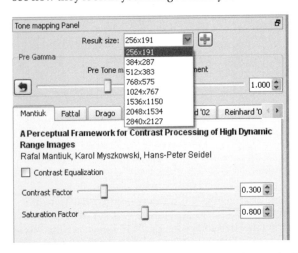

Figure 7-14. Changing the size of the output image in Qtpfsgui

Figure 7-15. Several previews using different operators in Qtpfsgui

Different operators will produce different effects in the image. Some of them were created with the objective of generating a realistic output. Some examples of these operators are Reinhard '02, Reinhard '05, Drago, and Durand. Other operators were created only with the idea of preserving the information of the original image, producing a more artistic effect, such as Mantiuk or Fattal. This artistic effect makes the photograph look somehow unrealistic but with a pleasant appearance. This kind of appearance has been so popular among some groups of photographers that to some people, HDR has become synonymous with unrealistic or dreamy images. Mantiuk, for example, produces interesting shadows and a unique look, especially nice when applied to a cloudy shot or to objects with a high level of texture. Fattal is by far the one that produces the most unrealistic images, yielding a soft colorful image that evokes fantasy or dreams. There are also a couple more operators, Ashikhmin and Pattanaik, that can also give good results but are not as popular as the previous ones.

Some operators are resolution-independent. This means that previewing the operator at smaller resolutions will give you a similar result when you use it at a larger resolution. Other operators are not resolution-independent, which means that they will produce different results when applied to different output resolutions, such as Fattal. The best thing to do in those cases is to preview with the exact size that you are going to work with.

Next, I will present these operators in more detail. I will show you the result of processing the example image of this chapter with every one of the operators, using the default settings at the largest resolution. Also, I will describe each of them, present the controls they offer, and explain how these controls can alter the resulting image.

Mantiuk

In his paper, Mantiuk states that this tone mapping operator was not designed for obtaining realistic images. The visual effects of this operator are very interesting, as it creates rich shadows as shown in

Figure 7-16. It is best-suited for artistic images rather than realistic images, although you can generate both types of images by changing the parameters accordingly (see Figure 7-17).

Figure 7-16. *This image shows the result of the Mantiuk tone mapping operator. Default settings were used. This produces dramatic shadows.*

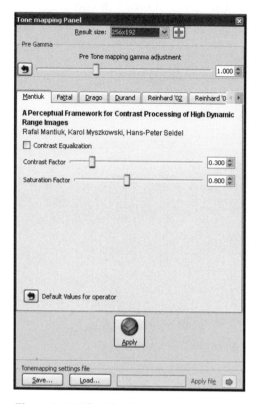

Figure 7-17. The Mantiuk tone mapping operator options in Qtpfsgui

There are three available controls for Mantiuk. The first one is called Contrast Equalization. You can enable or disable it. This control allows you to stretch the final image contrast, similar to what you can obtain by using Gimp later. The second control available is the Contrast Factor. If you increase this value, the shadow effect previously mentioned is decreased, obtaining a more realistic image, and vice versa. The Saturation Factor gives you control over how colorful the resulting image will be. If you increase this control, colors will be very intense, and if you decrease it, the image will look like grayscale.

Fattal

The Fattal operator is one of the most popular for creating artistic images, as shown in Figure 7-18. The resulting image is one of the closest to what many people call the "HDR look." Although, we all know by now that those images are in fact LDR images due to the tone mapping process.

Figure 7-18. This image shows the result of the Fattal tone mapping operator. Default settings were used. It provides a watercolor, or pencil-shaded, look.

There are five controls available in the Fattal operator, shown in Figure 7-19. The first parameter, Alpha, allows you to select the amount of detail enhancement. Higher values will produce images with more contrast and more shadows. Lower values will produce images with less contrast and shadows. The second parameter, Beta, controls how realistic the final image will be. Lower values of Beta produce highly unrealistic or watercolored images, while higher values produce more realistic colors in the image. The third parameter, Color Saturation, works similar as the Saturation Factor in Mantiuk: higher values produce colorful images and vice versa. The Noise Reduction parameter is for eliminating artifacts of the image. If you increase this value, the image tends to look more realistic. If you want artistic effects, keep this setting at zero or very low. Finally, the "Old" Fattal (pre 1.8.4) activates an older implementation of the algorithm. When this option is activated, it produces slightly more realistic outputs. It is recommended to uncheck this option if you want to achieve artistic effects. If you want to produce a realistic image, I recommended that you use another operator.

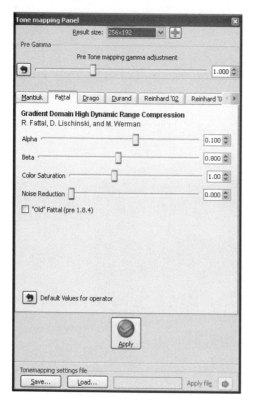

Figure 7-19. The Fattal tone mapping operator options in Qtpfsgui

Drago

The Drago operator is one of the simplest tone mapping operators to use. It is very fast and produces realistic images. You can see one example in Figure 7-20. This tone mapping operator is based on how humans perceive light. It uses luminance values under a logarithmic compression to reduce the dynamic range of the HDR image.

Figure 7-20. *This image shows the result of the Drago tone mapping operator. Default settings were used. This makes the image mostly mid-toned by providing overall balance.*

As Figure 7-21 shows, this operator only provides one control, Bias. This setting controls brightness, contrast, and level of details, all in just one slider. Lower values will produce brighter images with fewer details, while higher values decrease the brightness and increase the level of details. The resulting images are always realistic throughout the entire range of values of the Bias parameter; this means that you should not use this operator for artistic purposes.

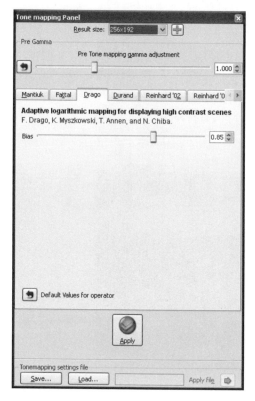

Figure 7-21. *The Drago tone mapping operator options in Qtpfsgui*

Durand

The Durand operator decomposes the HDR into two different layers, a base layer and a details layer. Contrast is reduced only in the base layer so that details are preserved. This operator only produces realistic images. You can see one example in Figure 7-22.

Figure 7-22. *This image shows the result of the Durand tone mapping operator. By default, it brings out the low end, but blows out the high end (highlights).*

This operator provides three different controls (see Figure 7-23); Spatial Kernel Sigma, Range Kernel Sigma, and Base Contrast. As stated by the authors in the original research paper, Spatial Kernel Sigma does not affect the final results much. They also recommend that the Range Kernel Sigma should be kept at 0.4, as they constantly obtained good results with that value. Finally, the Base Contrast controls the overall brightness and contrast of the image. Large values produce bright and high-contrasted images, while low values produce dark and low-contrasted images.

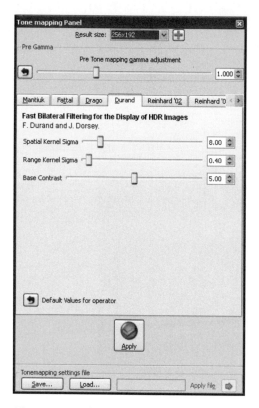

Figure 7-23. *The Durand tone mapping operator options in Qtpfsgui*

Reinhard '02

The Reinhard '02 tone mapping operator is one of the best for generating realistic images. It extends the work of Ansel Adams for dealing with digital images. An example of the result of this operator is shown in Figure 7-24.

Figure 7-24. *This image shows the result of the Reinhard '02 tone mapping operator. Default settings were used. This is the one I chose for the sample at the beginning of the chapter.*

This operator provides two interfaces, both shown in Figure 7-25: a simple one where only two parameters are needed and a more advanced where three extra parameters are included. To enable the advanced mode, select the Use Scales option. Increasing the Key Value produces brighter results, while decreasing it produces darker ones. Phi controls the level of sharpness in the image. Default values produce very good images.

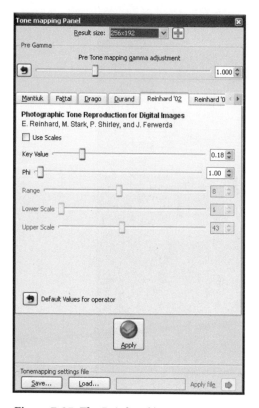

Figure 7-25. The Reinhard '02 tone mapping operator options in Qtpfsgui

Reinhard '05

The Reinhard '05 operator is similar to Reinhard '02, but this one is based on how the human visual system works. Although it produces realistic images, I would recommend Reinhard '02 over this one. You can see an example in Figure 7-26.

Figure 7-26. *This image shows the result of the Reinhard '05 tone mapping operator. Default settings were used. The results are very close to what could be seen in the original scene, just like the other Reinhard method .*

This operator allows you to control three parameters (see Figure 7-27): Brightness, Chromatic Adaptation, and Light Adaptation. The first one, Brightness, is self-explanatory; higher values produce brighter images, while lower values produce darker images. The second one, Chromatic Adaptation is kept at zero by the authors of the paper. Light Adaptation controls how sensible the algorithm is to light; increasing this value lightens dark areas.

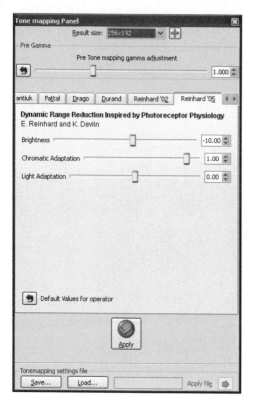

Figure 7-27. The Reinhard '05 tone mapping operator options in Qtpfsgui

Ashikhmin

The Ashikhmin operator uses a simplification of more elaborated models of the human visual system for reducing the color depth of the HDR image while keeping the details as much as possible, as Figure 7-28 shows.

Figure 7-28. This image shows the result of the Ashikhmin tone mapping operator. Default settings were used. This produces saturated colors and high mid-tones.

There are three parameters in this operator, shown in Figure 7-29: you can use the simple settings by enabling that option, or else you can select an equation and a Local Contrast Threshold. Low values of Local Contrast Threshold produce a softer and brighter image, while higher values produce a darker image with more details. Changing the equation number slightly changes the results.

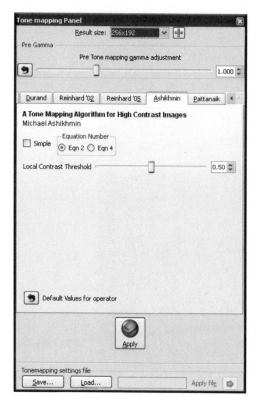

Figure 7-29. The Ashikhmin tone mapping operator options in Qtpfsgui

Pattanaik

The Pattanaik operator is a very complex operator that is based on the adaption of the visual system to the light over time. It tries to mimic how the human visual system works, as seen in Figure 7-30.

Figure 7-30. *This image shows the result of the Pattanaik tone mapping operator. Default settings produce an almost entirely white image, so I turned on the Local Tone Mapping option for this image. This produces high mid-tones.*

This operator is complex to use (see Figure 7-31). Enabling the Local Tone Mapping simplifies the process, yielding only one slider to set: the Multiplier. Lowering the value of this control will result in darker images, while increasing its value will result in brighter images. For more advanced control, you can disable the Local Tone Mapping and change the Cone and Rod level sliders. Enabling the Cone and Rod Based on Luminance option allows you to generate a more realistic image easier.

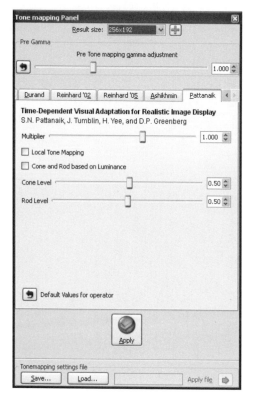

Figure 7-31. This image shows the Pattanaik tone mapping operator options in Qtpfsgui.

Summary

In this chapter, you learned how to create an HDR image from just a single RAW file or a set of LDR images. This allows you to capture virtually any scene with strong differences in illumination, resulting in a well-exposed photograph.

You also learned how to generate an LDR from the HDR image. This is very useful since most equipment only works with LDR images. We discussed several tone mapping operators for achieving different results, such as creating realistic images (that is, images that represent what a human observer would see at the scene), or artistic effects. As you can see from the examples in this chapter, results can vary widely based on the input images and the algorithm used to create the LDR image.

In the next chapter, I will show you how to fix different types of distortions present in your images produced by your lens and perspective.

CHAPTER 8

Distortion Correction

In photography, there are commonly two different sources of distortion. One of them is produced inside the camera, particularly in the lens. This distortion is called *lens distortion*. The other is produced by the relative position of the camera and the scene. This distortion is called *perspective distortion*. In this chapter, I will describe these two sources of distortion and show you how to correct them.

Lens Distortion Correction

Image distortion in a photograph is not uniform. The least distortion is present at the center of the image. Areas of the image closer to the borders show much more distortion than the center. This is explained because of the physical construction of the lens. Although theoretically possible, in practice it is not possible to construct a perfect lens. Keep in mind though that cheaper lenses present a much more evident distortion of the image than professional or more expensive lenses.

There are many different distortions that a lens can present, although two of the most common are radial distortion and vignetting.

Radial Distortion

Radial distortion commonly appears on digital photography, although in some cases it is much less noticeable than others due to the quality of the lens. One of the results of having a distorted image is that straight lines in the scene are bent in the image. This effect is much more noticeable in the edges of the image. This is especially problematic for architectural photography, where buildings and houses are expected to present many straight lines. Because of the distortion, many photographs do not look as professional as they should. Although in some cases the photographer may intentionally use this distortion as an artistic effect, in general, straight lines in the scene should be straight in the photograph as well.

This type of distortion presents the property that it is symmetrical; the farther apart the pixels are from the image center, the larger the distortion they have. The symmetrical shape of this distortion comes from the fact that lenses are symmetrical in the first place; they distort the image equally in every direction.

There are two different types of radial distortion: barrel and pincushion distortion.

Barrel Distortion

Think of *barrel distortion* as taking the corners of the image and bending them toward the center, shrinking the image, as Figure 8-1 shows. The visual effect of this distortion is that the image looks like it has been wrapped around a barrel, hence its name.

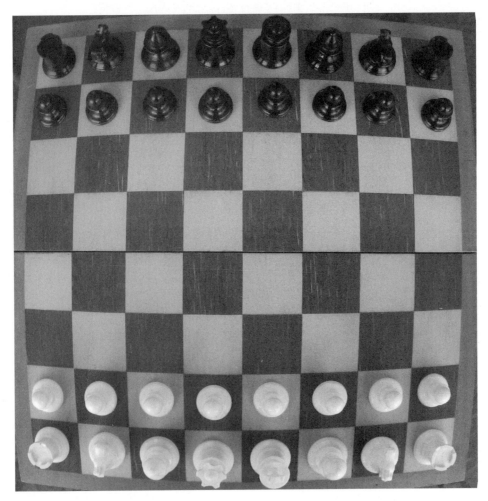

Figure 8-1. This image shows an exaggerated example of a barrel distortion.

Pincushion Distortion

The *pincushion distortion* is the opposite of the barrel distortion. Instead of shrinking, the image gets enlarged by bending the corners away from the center of the image, as you can see in Figure 8-2.

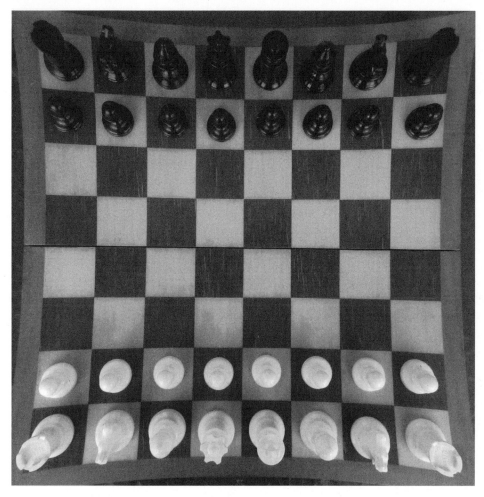

Figure 8-2. This image shows an exaggerated example of a pincushion distortion.

Vignetting

Vignetting is another kind of distortion present in some images. This distortion presents darker areas on the corners of the photograph, while the center is correctly bright, as shown in Figure 8-3. Many different things can cause this; a cheap lens, incorrect mounting of the lens, the use of stacked filters, among others. In some cases, it is just some external accessory of the camera blocking the light; in other cases, it can be a problem of the internal elements of the lens occluding themselves. In the latter case, you can solve this problem by reducing the aperture. This means that you need to select a larger F-number.

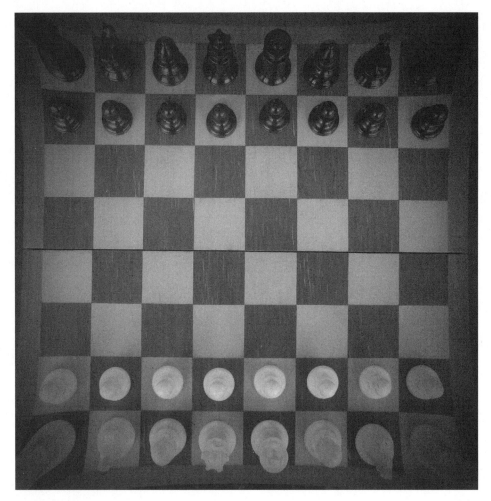

Figure 8-3. *This image shows an image that presents vignetting. Note how the corners of the image are darker than the center.*

Lens Distortion Correction with Gimp

Gimp offers a feature that allows you to correct these two types of distortions. This feature is called Lens Distortion Correction. To access the Lens Distortion Correction dialog box in the Gimp (see Figure 8-4), select Filters → Distorts → Lens Distortion.

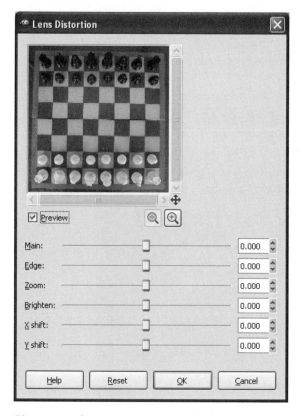

Figure 8-4. The Lens Distortion dialog box in Gimp

There are six parameters that you can change in the Lens Distortion dialog box. Each of them control a specific part of the lens distortion being applied to the image.

The first parameter, Main, allows you to apply a radial distortion to the image. Negative numbers mean that a pincushion distortion is being applied, and positive numbers indicate that a barrel distortion is being applied. In both cases, the magnitude of this value represents how strong the distortion is. The idea is to apply the inverse distortion that the image currently has so that the final image does not present any distortion. The way to correct barrel distortion is to apply pincushion distortion, and vice versa. This will result in the straight lines in the scene being represented using straight lines in the image as well.

The second parameter, named Edge, produces the same effects as the Main parameter, only that it is applied mainly in the borders of the image, leaving the center untouched. This may be useful when large bent lines are in the border and you do not want to alter the image center.

The third parameter is called Zoom. Because radial distortion alters the size of the image, you can use this option to zoom in or out. Barrel distortion makes the image smaller, while a pincushion distortion makes the image larger. Note that this zoom parameter is not only a visualization tool; it will produce changes in the image itself.

The Brighten parameter allows you to reduce the vignetting distortion. This option allows you to brighten up the edges, especially the corners of the image. Note that this feature only works when the

Main or the Edge parameters have a value set different from zero. If both are set to zero, this parameter does not make any change to the image.

The fifth and sixth parameters, X and Y shift, represent the center of the effect. The default value is the center of the image. Some distortions are not centered in the exact middle of the image; therefore, changing these parameters allows you to correct those problems accordingly. As an example, I will show you how to solve a barrel distortion problem, starting with Figure 8-5.

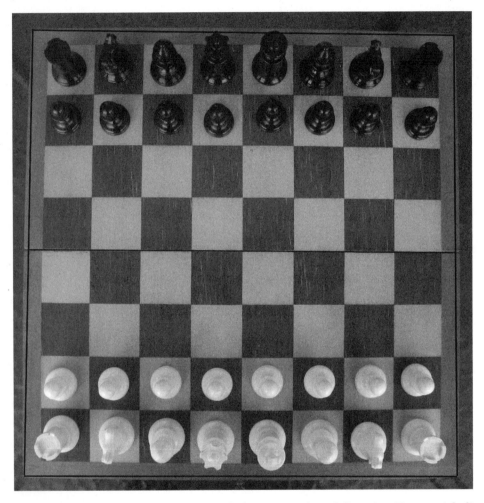

Figure 8-5. This image shows a photograph that presents barrel distortion. Four straight lines were added to the image to show that the edges of the chessboard are bent.

The objective in this case is to use a pincushion distortion in the Lens Distortion dialog box so that the straight lines of the scene are kept straight in the image.

If you move the Main slider to the left, you will apply a pincushion distortion to the image; or in other words, you will reduce the barrel distortion on the image. You need to use the preview window and move the slider until you see straight lines. If you apply more than enough for removing the barrel distortion, the image will start looking like it had pincushion distortion in the first place, as shown in Figure 8-6.

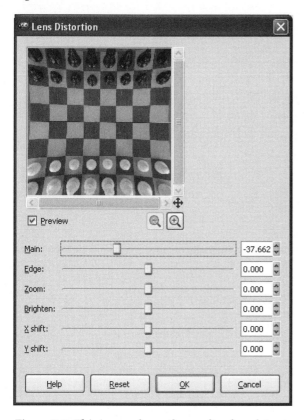

Figure 8-6. *This image shows the results of applying too much pincushion distortion to correct a barrel distortion.*

If you move the slider to the wrong side, you will be applying the same barrel distortion that the image had, increasing the effect.

You can see in this example how the barrel distortion shrinks the image. It is in these cases where you can use the Zoom parameter accommodate the image into the desired level of zoom so that only the usable part of the image remains, as shown in Figure 8-7.

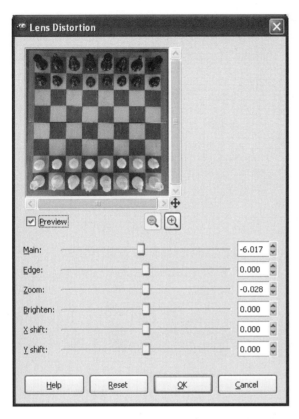

Figure 8-7. *This image shows the settings used in the Lens Distortion dialog box in Gimp for correcting the barrel distortion.*

After you select the proper parameters and click OK, you should have a corrected image, as Figure 8-8 shows. You can check with the Measure tool if the lines are now straight in the final image. Remember that you can undo this effect and try again as many times as you want. You can undo this, or any other step in Gimp, by pressing Ctrl+Z, or selecting Edit → Undo.

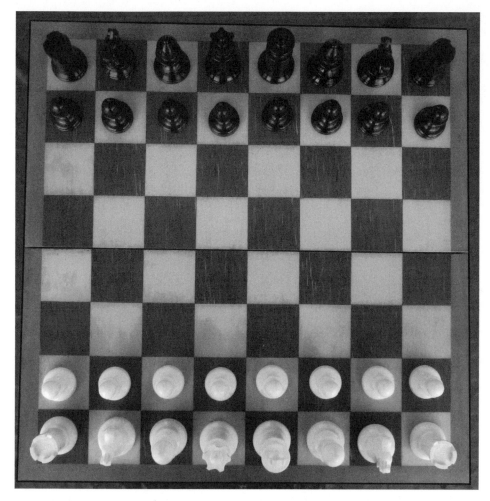

Figure 8-8. *This image shows that the lines are now straight. This is confirmed by adding artificial straight black lines.*

Now I will show you how to solve a case where vignetting occurred, such as the one shown in Figure 8-3.

In Gimp, you need to set the value of the Main or the Edge slider to a value other than zero in order to make the vignetting reduction work. In this case, I chose a value of -20 for the Main slider, as Figure 8-9 shows. This means that I am applying a pincushion distortion, but because the initial image presented some barrel distortion, it will correct how the image looks. The second parameter that you need to use is the Zoom. Because you are changing the size of the image by applying a distortion, you need to zoom in or out, depending on the effect. Finally, you can select the level of Brightness, which lightens up the dark corners, reducing the vignetting effect.

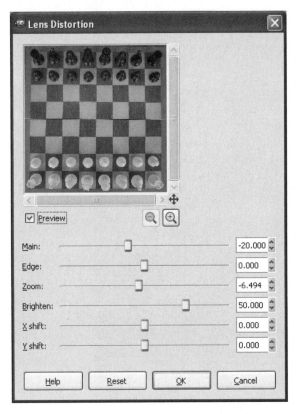

Figure 8-9. This image shows the parameters needed for reducing the effect of vignetting.

By using Gimp, you can manually fix distortions in the lens, such as radial distortion and vignetting, by changing the parameters in the Lens Distortion dialog box.

Perspective Distortion Correction

In some situations, you may not be able to take a picture in the exact angle of view that you wanted. This may be caused by the existence of objects blocking your way or it may be impossible or very hard to position the camera exactly in front of the subject center. When the camera is not parallel with the subject, a certain degree of perspective distortion appears. A common case of this problem appears when you try to photograph a building at street level, as shown in Figure 8-10; every floor of the building appears in the image with a different size and angle caused by the perspective distortion. On the other hand, you may actually want to introduce some distortion to emphasize height. In either case we use the same tool.

As you may already know by now, a photograph is a two-dimensional projection of a three-dimensional world. Using mathematical formulas, you can re-project this view into another one, obtaining a similar image that you could have obtained by just moving the camera before taking the photograph, as shown in Figure 8-11.

Changing the view of a scene is a general change. Resizing, rotating, and other geometric transforms are subsets of it. This means that you are able to achieve all those effects with just this correction. Although it is possible, I suggest that you keep using the other tools for simpler geometric transforms since they are easier to operate.

Figure 8-10. This image shows the original picture of a building. It clearly shows perspective distortion. Note how every floor appears as a different size in the image.

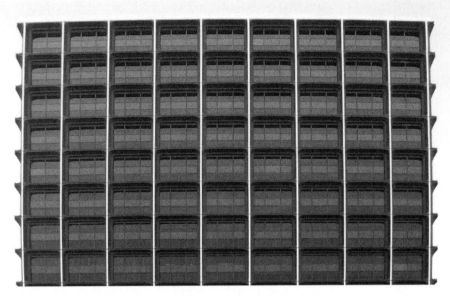

Figure 8-11. This image shows the result of perspective correction. Note how every floor has the same size and the lines are vertical and horizontal now.

Perspective Distortion Correction Using Gimp

Gimp provides a very useful tool for correcting perspective distortion. To open the Perspective tool in Gimp, select Tools → Transform Tools → Perspective. Also, you can access it by selecting its icon from the Toolbox window, as shown in Figure 8-12.

Figure 8-12. This image shows how to access the Perspective tool in Gimp.

Once you select the Perspective tool in Gimp, you need to make sure that in the Toolbox window, under the Perspective section (see Figure 8-13), the Direction parameter is set to Corrective (Backward) and the Preview is set to Image + Grid. Also, it is important that the Interpolation parameter is set to Cubic or Sinc so that the image quality does not degrade so much. Refer to Chapter 3 if you don't know what Cubic or Sinc interpolation is.

Figure 8-13. The Perspective section of the Toolbox. Make sure that Corrective (Backward) is selected under Direction and that Preview is set to Image + Grid.

After settings those parameters, you need to click once on the image, which will generate the initial grid lines shown in Figure 8-14.

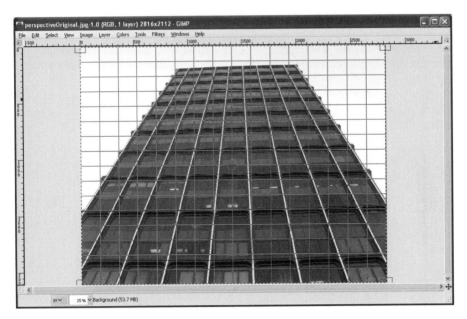

Figure 8-14. This image shows the initial grid lines of the Perspective tool in Gimp.

You can start dragging the corners of the grid lines so that you get a feel for how they move. The idea is to represent the perspective distortion present in the image with the grid lines. This means that you need to adjust the grid so that its lines pass exactly along, or at least are parallel to, the straight lines in the image, as shown in Figure 8-15. If you feel that you need more or less grid lines to achieve more precision, you can adjust the Number of grid lines parameter under the Perspective section in the Toolbox. Also, you can always zoom in so that you get a larger representation of a specific area by holding Ctrl while rotating the mouse wheel up.You can also control zoom by going into View → Zoom and choosing the specific zoom level you are interested in, as well as by using the Zoom tool.

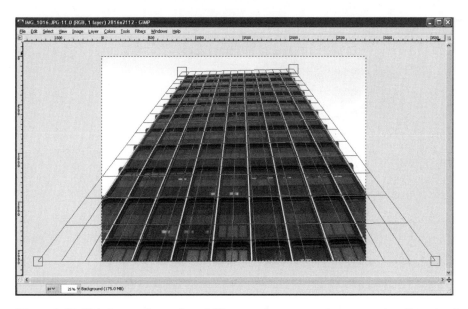

Figure 8-15. *This image shows the grid lines used to correct the perspective distortion in this case. The lines of the image that are parallel to the grid lines will become vertical or horizontal lines in the processed image.*

Once you have the grid lines correctly placed, you only need to press the Enter key. This will start the perspective correction process. Once this process is finished, the image will be free of perspective distortion, as Figure 8-16 shows.

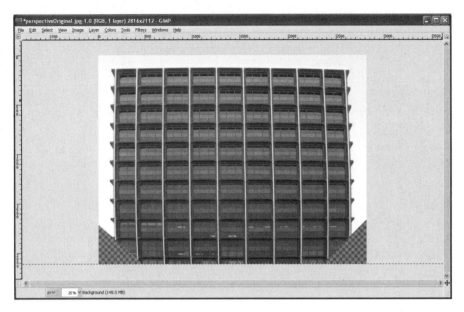

Figure 8-16. *This image shows the result of the perspective distortion correction tool in Gimp.*

As you can see from Figure 8-16, when you correct the perspective of an image, there will be some areas that do not have information. One option to solve this is to crop the image so that the areas that do not present information are deleted. Just use the Crop tool to remove the unwanted areas, as shown in Figure 8-17.

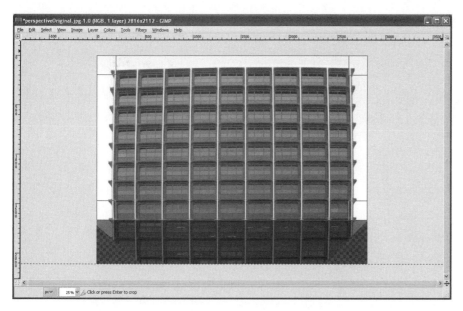

Figure 8-17. This image shows how to crop the areas where no information is present.

Another technique that you can use in some cases is to fill the areas that do not present information. You can do this with the Resynthesizer plug-in or with the Clone tool from Chapter 6 that I used for object removal. This technique works very well with textures such as sand, grass, sky, water, and so forth, but it does not produce very good results when there are structured objects as in the previous image.

Correcting Perspective Distortions with Shear

There is a simpler tool for correcting smaller perspective distortions. It is called Shear tool. You can select it by going into Tools → Transform Tools → Shear. You can also access it by selecting its icon in the Toolbox, as shown in Figure 8-18. You can see an image that I will fix with the Shear tool in Figure 8-19.

Figure 8-18. *Accessing the SheartTool in Gimp.*

Figure 8-19. *This image shows an example of perspective distortion. Note how the building looks like it is slanted.*

After you select the Shear tool, just click on the image and the Shear tool dialog box will appear, as shown in Figure 8-20. In there, you can set the magnitude of the Shear effect in the X and Y axes. You can only set one axis at a time. If you need the effect in both axes, you will need to run the Shear tool twice.

If you put a positive number in the X axis, the top of the image will move to the left and the bottom to the right, and vice versa for negative numbers. In the Y axis, if you put a positive number, the left part of the image will move up, and the right part will move down, and vice versa for negative numbers. In all cases, the absolute value represents the magnitude of the effect.

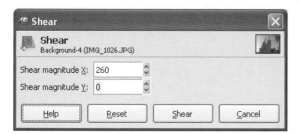

Figure 8-20. This image shows the Shear tool dialog and the settings used to straighten the building.

You can see the results of the Shear tool in Figure 8-21. You can crop the result, or use what you learned from Chapter 6 to add texture where it is missing.

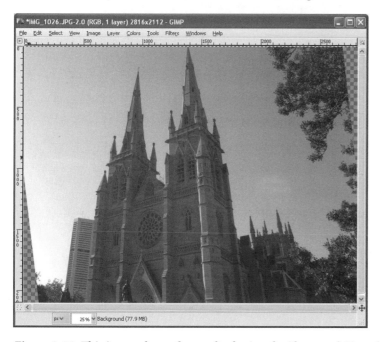

Figure 8-21. This image shows the result of using the Shear tool. Now the building does not look slanted any more.

203

After removing some distracting objects and filling in the areas that don't have information, the image now looks like that in Figure 8-22.

Figure 8-22. This image shows the final result of using the Shear tool. Note that areas were filled with the Clone and Heal tools. Read Chapter 6 for more info on those tools.

Summary

In this chapter, you learned how to correct the distortions usually caused by the lens: radial distortion and vignetting. Also, you are now able to correct perspective distortions caused by the positioning of the camera.

In the next chapter, you will learn how to create great-looking panoramas.

■ ■ ■

CHAPTER 9

Panorama Photo Stitching

A panorama is an image that represents a much larger field of view than a regular image. You can use them for many purposes, such as banners, newsletter separators, posters, or web site headers. In many cases, you cannot capture the entire scene in a single shot with a regular camera. One of those cases can be, for example, when you try to take a photograph of a very tall or wide building. In those cases, you can create a panorama by just taking many regular photographs of the scene and then stitch them on your computer to create a single panoramic image. Note that creating a panorama with this method results in an image with larger resolution than a regular shot so you will also be able to make larger prints from it.

Capturing a Panorama

The first step in creating a panorama is to take the individual photos that are going to be stitched into the panorama. These photographs have to be taken from the same point of perspective. This is very important because if you move the camera to another position, it may be impossible to stitch the panorama.

For you to understand what I mean by taking the photographs from the same point of perspective, I will use the human body as an analogy. When you look at any scene and move your head from one side to the other, you can see that the position of the objects that are closer to you changes faster than the position of the objects that are far away. If you stand still and only move your eyes, the position of the objects remains the same. This is because the eyes move around their optical center, thus no change in perspective occurs. That is exactly what you need to do to take good photographs for a panorama, rotate the camera around its optical center, just like the eyes do.

To rotate your camera exactly around its optical axis, you will need a sturdy tripod and a panoramic head. A panoramic head is special hardware that connects to your tripod and allows you to define the specific axis of rotation that your camera needs so that it maintains the same point of perspective while rotating it in any angle.

Do not worry if you do not have a panoramic head, you can still make some types of panoramas. If the panorama that you want to photograph has close subjects, you will need the panoramic head because small errors in the angle of rotation will produce large differences in perspective in those subjects. On the other hand, if your subjects are far away, you do not need a panoramic head because small changes in the angle of rotation produce very small errors in the perspective of those subjects. In the latter case, you can use a simple tripod, or even take the photos handheld.

Start the process by designing how are you going to take the photographs. Is it a horizontal or vertical panorama? It can also be both. You can mentally organize your photos into rows and columns. Maybe you only need one row of images for a horizontal panorama. Or maybe the buildings are taller than you thought and you will be using two rows instead of one. Try different angles and see how much of the scene you can cover in every shot.

As a general rule of thumb for a good panorama, every image should overlap at least a third with the previous image. If you can overlap more than a third, it will produce better results. Keep in mind, though, that the number of required images will increase if you increase the size of the overlapping regions. Because the computer will try to match every image using control points, it is very important to try to make the overlap where a lot of texture is present. This means that areas with a lot of details or contrast are good areas for overlapping. On the other hand, areas with poor contrast or detail, such as a completely blue sky, for instance, are bad areas for overlapping because every pixel will look the same for the computer and it will not be able to match the images. Also, moving areas such as tree branches in high winds are not good because they may change position from one image to the other. Try to keep any moving object isolated in just one shot.

Timing is also important. You should take all your images quickly so that the illumination does not change so much. This is especially critical at sunrise and sunset, when just a couple of minutes make a lot of change in illumination.

In general, you should maintain all the controls the same while taking the images. You should use the same focal length (zoom) and focal point.

Once you are done with the design, you can proceed to the next step: taking the photographs.

Take the first shot that covers a limited part of the scene. Then rotate the camera so that it covers the next position and continue until you have every part of the scene covered. Remember to be methodic in taking the photographs; you can start from left to right until you finish the first row and then go down to the next one. You do not want to come back home and see that you missed one spot. It is also important that you use the same camera settings for every shot; white balance, aperture, iso, and exposure time. Some cameras have a stitching mode where they lock these settings with the first shot. You can also use the manual mode for locking these settings. In general, I don't recommend that you use the automatic mode, because the exposure will change drastically in every shot.

Once you have taken all your images, you can stitch them together in your computer, creating a single image that covers the entire scene. Figures 9-1 through 9-5 show an example of a horizontal panorama using four images.

Figure 9-1. This is the first image used for stitching.

Figure 9-2. This is the second image used for stitching.

Figure 9-3. This is the third image used for stitching.

Figure 9-4. This is the fourth image used for stitching.

Figure 9-5. This image shows the final panorama created by stitching the four separate images.

Image Projections

There are different image projections that you can choose for creating your panorama. This depends on the field of view of the scene that you want to cover. Although there are many different projections that you can apply to a panorama, two of them are the most commonly used: rectilinear and cylindrical projection.

Rectilinear projection is one of the most popular choices when creating a horizontal panorama. One of the advantages of this projection is that vertical and horizontal straight lines in the real world remain straight in the panorama. The main disadvantage of this projection is that when you produce an image with a large field of view, objects at the edges of the image become very distorted so that they can remain straight. This translates into exaggerated sizes of these objects. You should only use this projection if you want to produce a horizontal panorama that encompasses a field of view of less than 120 degrees.

The cylindrical projection allows you to stitch horizontal panoramas with a field of view of up to 360 degrees. One advantage of this projection is that vertical straight lines from the real world are straight in the panorama. Also, when the panoramas have 360 degrees, you can create a continuous panorama; the left-most part of it is connected to the right-most part. You can use this, for example, as a matte in a computer-generated scene.

Creating Panoramas With Hugin

The program that I am going to use to create panoramas is called Hugin. It is great software started by Pablo d'Angelo and now released under the GNU Public License. You can read the Appendix for instruction on how to download and install it.

I will show you how easy it is to create a simple panorama and then I will show you the different options that are available while creating a more complex one.

After you open Hugin, the first step is to load the images that you are going to stitch together to create the panorama. To do that, you need to press the Load images button shown in Figure 9-6.

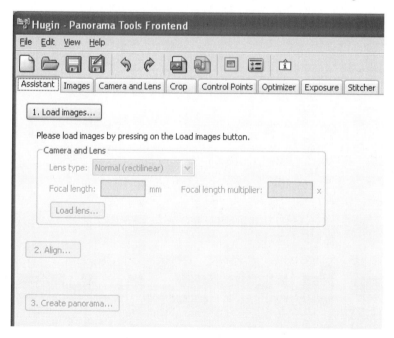

Figure 9-6. This image shows the initial screen of the Hugin software.

A dialog box will appear asking where the images are. You need to select all of the images that you want to use to create the panorama, as shown in Figure 9-7. You can select one by one by holding the Ctrl key on your keyboard while clicking on each photo, or you can select all of them at once by just clicking the mouse and then moving it so that the selection encompasses all of them.

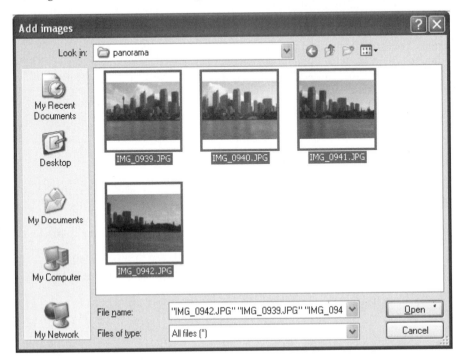

Figure 9-7. This image shows how to select all the images in Hugin.

After loading the images, the Align button in the main window will become active, as Figure 9-8 shows. You need to press that button so that Hugin starts automatically aligning all the images for you. This process may take several minutes to complete because the computations that Hugin needs to perform are intensive. The processing time depends, among other things, on the number of images that you loaded; the more images you want to align, the larger the processing time will be.

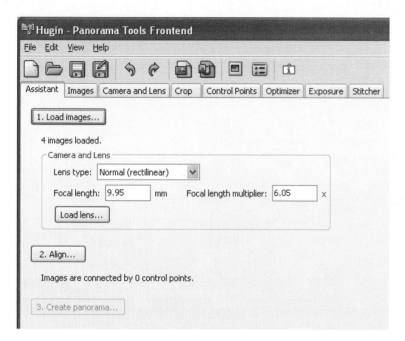

Figure 9-8. *This is the main window of Hugin. Note how the Align button is enabled after loading the images*

After Hugin finishes aligning your images, a new window will appear, showing you a preview of your panorama, as shown in Figure 9-9. You can close this window for now; in the next section, I will show you some of these options.

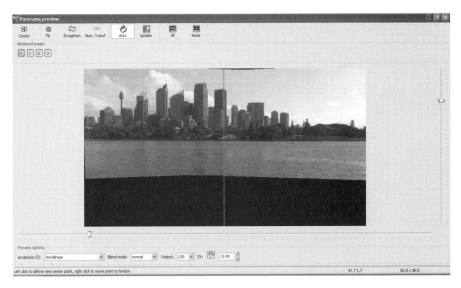

Figure 9-9. *This image shows the output of the stitching process. Note that rectilinear projection was selected because of the small field of view. It has the nice property of maintaining straight lines straight.*

In the main window, the Create panorama button is now enabled (Figure 9-10). This means that everything is ready to generate and save your panorama. Press that button so that you can save your panorama.

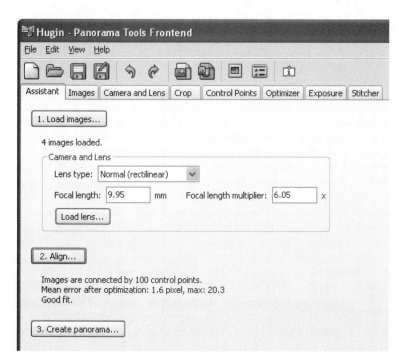

Figure 9-10. This image shows the main window of Hugin. After aligning the images, the Create panorama button is enabled, allowing you to save the final image.

After you press the Create panorama button, a dialog box will appear asking for an output prefix. You need to enter the name and location for your panorama image. You cannot specify a file type here because Hugin will use its default file type, which is TIFF. After you've selected the output, you'll see a window showing the output of the stitching process (Figure 9-11).

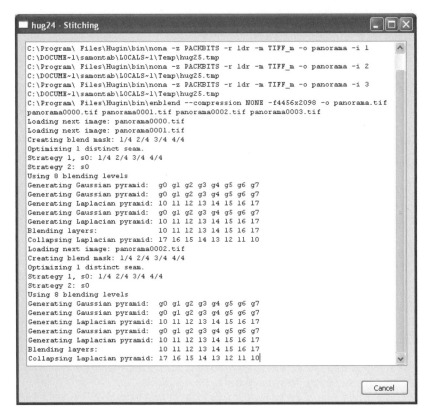

Figure 9-11. This image shows the output of the stitching process in Hugin. When this is finished, your panorama will be saved where you specified.

The last step is to crop or fill the image so that it is shown as a regular photograph. Open the panorama image with Gimp (see Figure 9-12). The default image type used in Hugin is TIFF, so in this example, the file name of the panorama is `panorama.tif`.

Figure 9-12. This image shows how a panorama looks before cropping.

Regular Crop

Select the Cropping tool and select the largest rectangle that does not contain any invisible areas. You may need to zoom in and examine all four sides of the rectangle to make sure that only visible information is inside (see Figure 9-13). Remember that you can adjust the sides of the cropping selection by dragging them. If you are wondering which aspect ratio to use, I suggest you to use a standard one, such as 16:9, which is high definition video; 2.4:1, which is anamorphic; or even 4:1, which is exactly six standard 35mm films side by side. Another option is to just crop to the specific use of the image.

Figure 9-13. This image shows the resulting image after cropping a panorama in Gimp.

The regular crop will work with any type of image, although you may need to cut too much information in some cases, leaving a very small image in the end. This effect is more accentuated when the camera was also moved to another angle, vertically in this case, when the images were taken.

Crop With Filling

One option to not sacrifice valuable information in the images is to fill the gaps. You can do this by using the Resynthesizer plug–in, or the Clone and Heal tools that I have used in Chapter 6. This technique works best for textures such as sky, water, grass, and so forth.

The first step is to remove the excess of invisible pixels. You can do that by just going to Image → Autocrop Image. This function will crop the image into a rectangle that holds all the pixels with information. This means that this rectangle will also contain some invisible pixels, which are the ones that I will show you how to fill next.

The next step is to select all the invisible pixels remaining. You can do that by going to Select → By Color. Then, you only need to click on one invisible pixel and all of them will be selected. After this, you can proceed as explained in Chapter 6.

The final result can be substantially larger than the regular crop, but in some types of images, it may not produce good results due to difficult textures such as well-defined objects. You may try to use the crop with filling first and if you are not able to fill the gaps, you can just use the regular crop for that area. Figure 9-14 shows the final result.

Figure 9-14. *This image shows the final panorama using crop with filling. There is a slightly larger portion of water and sky.*

In this example, the crop with filling produced an image seven percent larger than the one produced with the regular crop. This difference is small in this example because the camera was correctly aligned using a tripod during the shots. Also, in this example, only four images were used, so the errors in alignment could not propagate much. When taking more images or when the camera is not correctly aligned while taking the photos, this difference can be larger. Even with this small difference, it is always recommended to use crop with filling whenever possible to increase the size of the resulting panorama.

Creating More Complex Panoramas

In the previous section, I showed you how to stitch simple panoramas. That technique uses a rectilinear projection. By using that technique, you can easily stitch together many images, preserving the look of a regular photograph; straight lines in the real world remain straight in the image. Although, as I stated earlier, if the resulting field of view is larger than around 120 degrees, the objects at the edges will look bad.

In this section, I will show you how to create a panorama using a cylindrical projection so that the panorama can encompass up to 360 degrees horizontally. Also, in this panorama, I used two rows of images, each one covering 360 degrees horizontally. I did that to capture the trees and the top of the buildings as well.

If you use a rectilinear projection for this example where a field of view of 360 degrees was used, the resulting panorama will not look good. This is because the edges of the image will be extremely distorted. Figure 9-15 shows this example using the rectilinear projection. Note how the edges of the panorama are extremely distorted and the central part is too small to be visible in this field of view.

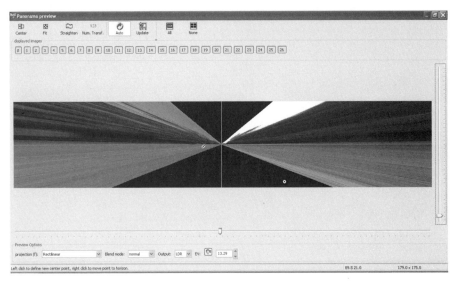

Figure 9-15. This image shows the rectilinear projection of a panorama with a field of view of 360 degrees horizontally. Note the extreme distortion of the objects at the edges caused by the large field of view.

Using the cylindrical projection allows you to have a field of view of up to 360 degrees, as shown in Figure 9-16. The main drawback of this projection is that horizontal straight lines in the real world are bent in the resulting panorama. On the other hand, vertical straight lines and the relative size of the objects in the image are preserved. You can select the cylindrical projection from the drop-down menu in the lower left part of the window.

Figure 9-16. This image shows the same panorama using the cylindrical projection.

In this dialog box, you can alter some other parameters of the panorama apart from its projection. If you click with the left button on any pixel of the image, it becomes the new center of the panorama, as shown in Figure 9-17. If you right-click on any pixel, that specific pixel will be projected to the horizon (the horizontal white line in the center), as Figure 9-18 shows. You can also manipulate the horizontal and vertical field of view of the resulting panorama by moving the horizontal and vertical sliders. You can also click on the Center, Fit, or Straighten buttons to automatically align the panorama if you feel lost with the manual controls.

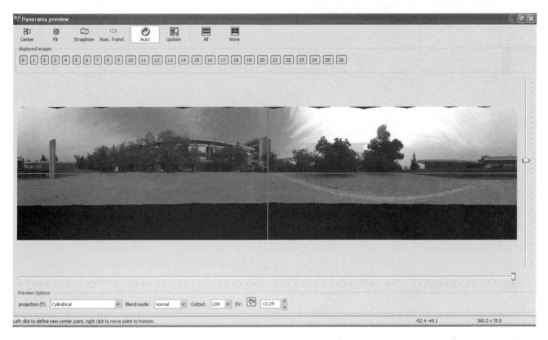

Figure 9-17. *This image shows the same panorama but centered in another spot. You can change the center of the panorama by just clicking the left button in that point.*

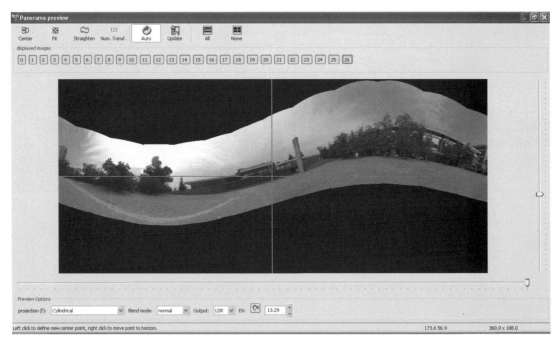

Figure 9-18. *This image shows the result of moving some points to the horizon. You can alter the view in many different ways using these manual controls. Pressing the Straighten button turns this image back into its original shape.*

Also, you can toggle on or off each one of the images being used to generate the panorama by clicking on its number. In this example, there are 27 images being used, numbered from 0 to 26. The images 0 to 13 are the first row of images, covering the ground. The rest of the images cover the sky and the top of both the trees and the buildings. As an example, Figure 9-19 shows the panorama without the top row images.

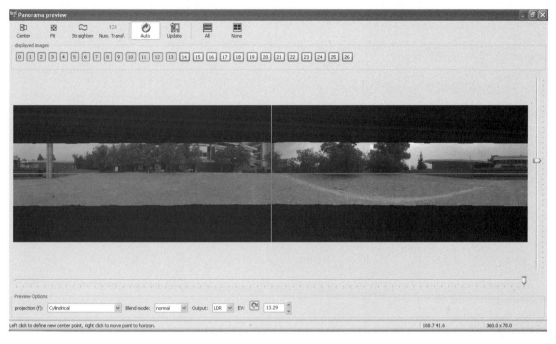

Figure 9-19. *This image shows the result of turning off all the images from the top row, which are the images 14 to 26 in this case.*

Once you are happy with the panorama that you want to create, you can press the Stitch now button from the Stitcher tab or click on the Create panorama button from the Assistant tab. Then you can proceed as before with the cropping/filling for the finishing touches. You can see the resulting image in Figure 9-20.

Figure 9-20. *The final result of the panorama*

Other Projections

There are some other image projections that you can use for more artistic effects or for other applications. Next, I will show you two of the most popular ones, fisheye and stereographic projections.

Creating a Metal Sphere With Hugin

The fisheye projection generates an image that looks like a metal sphere with the reflections of the scene, as shown in Figure 9-21. You can use this type of projection in computer-generated scenes to simulate global illumination from an environment, and to fake reflections that you would encounter in a real world. It is also known as an Angular Map.

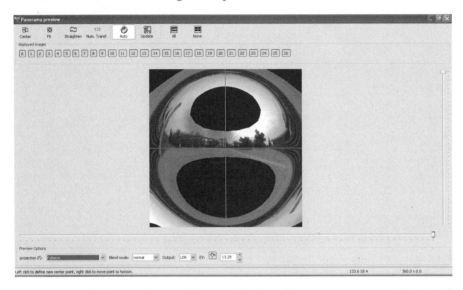

Figure 9-21. This image shows a fisheye projection of the same panorama. The visual aspect of this projection is like the scene is being seen through a metal sphere.

Note that there are two large holes in the example image. This is because this type of projections needs more images. It needs the panoramic image to cover a field of view of 360 degrees horizontally and 180 degrees vertically. This means that you have to take many pictures, from the ground up to the sky.

Creating a Little Planet With Hugin

You can use the stereographic projection in Hugin to create what are referred to as "little planets." This technique has been very popular in online photo sites. To create a good little planet, you will need a panoramic image that encompasses a field of view of 360 degrees horizontally and 180 degrees vertically. This means that you have to take a lot of photographs; shooting from pointing completely down to the ground to pointing up to the sky, and all in between. If you take fewer photographs, as in the case of this example, you will end up with holes in your planet.

To obtain good results, you need to have three well-defined horizontal areas in your panorama. At the very top, you will need a good portion of clear sky without any objects. At the center, you will have objects that may be trees, buildings, or other things. Finally, at the bottom, you should have the ground. I recommended that you don't capture any objects on the ground, because it's going to be heavily distorted. Just get some regular texture such as grass, sand, concrete, and the like.

To create the little planet, you need to use a stereographic projection. In the preview panorama window, select Stereographic from the projection drop-down menu, as shown in Figure 9-22. While using the stereographic projection, you can only control one slider, the horizontal one. If you move it to the right, you zoom out, and if you move it to the left, you zoom in. Clicking with the left button on any pixel will center the image at that point. To create these little planets, make sure that the center is in the ground area, or at least where it is supposed to be as in this example. Right-clicking on any pixel will move that pixel down or up into the horizontal line in the center. This will cause a rotation of the planet. The farther away from the horizontal line you right-click, the larger the rotation of the planet. Once you are happy with how your planet looks, you can proceed to stitch the panorama with the same steps used previously in this chapter.

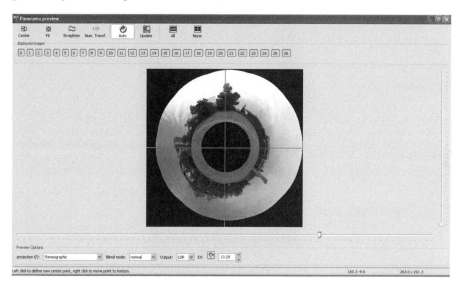

Figure 9-22. The stereographic projection in Hugin for creating a little planet

After you stitch the panorama, you can open it with Gimp and process it further. You could, for example, fill the holes if you missed some images. Go to Chapter 6 for more information on this.

Creating a Little Planet With Gimp

If you did not capture all the needed images for this projection, which are a lot, you can still make a little planet with the help of Gimp. First, you need to make the regular panorama with the cylindrical projection and then crop the results into a rectangle. You should have an image similar to the one in Figure 9-20. Open it in Gimp and go to Filters → Distorts → Polar Coordinates. A dialog box will appear with the options for this effect, as shown in Figure 9-23.

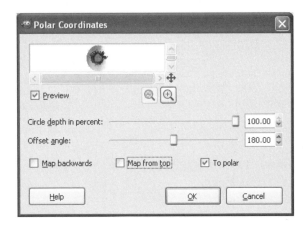

Figure 9-23. The Polar Coordinates filter

There are only two options that really matter for this effect: Offset angle and Map from top. The Offset angle allows you to rotate your planet. You can check it in the preview window. The Map from top option tells Gimp which part of the image will be in the center of the new image. If your panorama has the sky on top and the ground at the bottom, which most will, you need to uncheck the Map from top option so that the ground becomes the center of the planet. If your image is inverted, you should leave this option checked. After you apply the effect, you should see something similar to Figure 9-24.

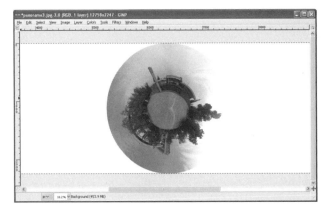

Figure 9-24. This image shows the resulting image after applying the Polar Coordinates distortion in Gimp.

Later, you can crop and edit your image so that you finish with something like Figure 9-25.

Figure 9-25. This image shows the final result of a little planet done with Gimp.

Hugin Options

Until now, I have shown you how to use the assistant in Hugin, which simplifies the process of creating a panorama. Note that you can produce all the previous effects with just the assistant. If you want more control in the process of stitching the panorama, you can access the other tabs of the program. Now I will show you what you can control with these tabs.

The Images tab contains the information about the individual images used to generate the panorama, as shown in Figure 9-26. For every image, it shows the number of control points found. Here, you can add or remove individual images for creating the panorama. You may want to remove images that have a low number of control points or that produce bad results in the stitched image because they have a different exposure or contain a moving object, for example.

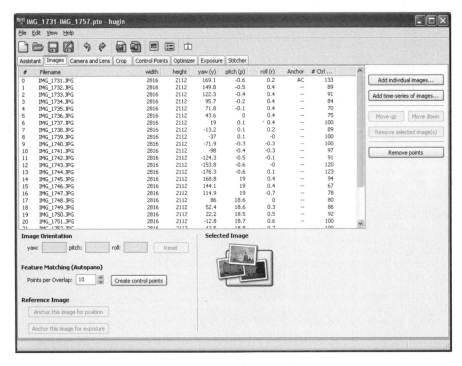

Figure 9-26. This image shows the Images tab in Hugin.

On the Camera and Lens tab, shown in Figure 9-27, you can save, load, or edit the lens information for every single one of the photographs that you are going to use in the panorama. Also, you can load EXIF metadata for each one of them.

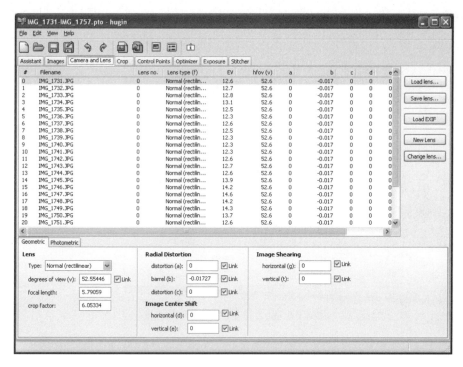

Figure 9-27. This image shows the Camera and Lens tab in Hugin.

There is a Crop tab in the main window that allows you to crop any of the images that are going to be stitched. Figure 9-28 shows this tab.

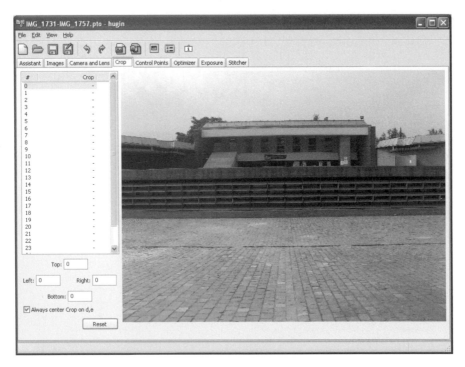

Figure 9-28. This image shows the Crop tab in Hugin.

On the Control Points tab, you can see all the control points calculated by Hugin. On this tab, shown in Figure 9-29, you can check, add, or erase the control points of any pair of images of the panorama. Manually added control points are useful when the automatic align tool is not working correctly.

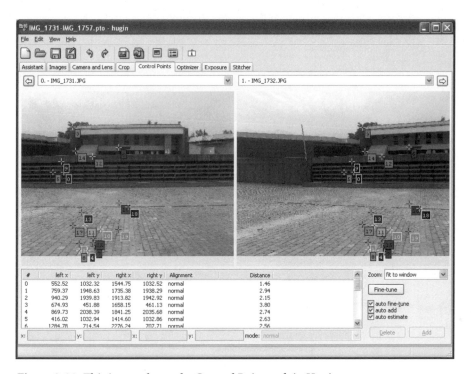

Figure 9-29. This image shows the Control Points tab in Hugin.

You can manually add a control point by first selecting two adjacent images, then clicking on one feature in the left image and clicking on the same feature on the right image. As you can see in Figure 9-30, Hugin preferred to select control points from rigid structures such as the floor or buildings rather than the tree, which may have moved in between the shots.

Figure 9-30. This image shows a different set of control points in Hugin.

To delete a control point, you only need to select it and then click the Delete button, as shown in Figure 9-31.

Figure 9-31. This image shows how to delete a control point.

The Optimizer tab in the main window, shown in Figure 9-32, allows you to select what action you want to perform with the images. You can use it to correct distortion, straighten up lines, or stitch images together. You can select what you want to do from the Optimize drop-down menu.

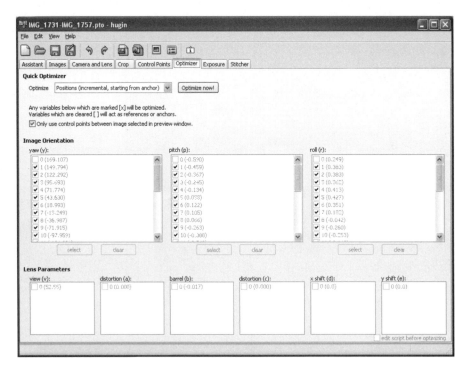

Figure 9-32. This image shows the Optimizer tab in Hugin.

The Exposure tab allows you to configure Hugin to correct vignetting problems as well as blending images with different exposures. As you can see from Figure 9-33, the assistant selected the necessary options for correcting vignetting.

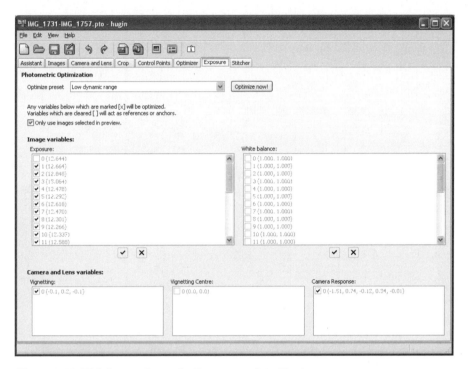

Figure 9-33. *This image shows the Exposure tab in Hugin.*

On the Stitcher tab, shown in Figure 9-34, you can select the file format of your panorama, along many other options. In the lower right part of the dialog, there is a drop-down menu called Normal Output. The default is TIFF, but you can change it to PNG or JPG.

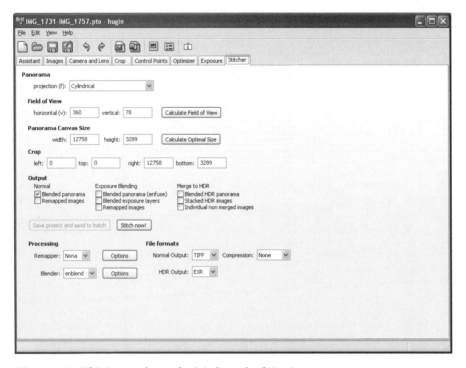

Figure 9-34. This image shows the Stitcher tab of Hugin.

Note that for regular use of this software, such as producing the effects I showed you earlier, the assistant will change all the parameters in the other tabs for you. In general, you should not need to manually change these settings. On the other hand, if you want advanced use of this software, such as automatically correcting distortions, these tabs are the place to go.

Summary

In this chapter, you learned how to make panoramas. You learned about projections and which one you should use depending on your needs. You learned that for regular panoramas, you should use either rectilinear or cylindrical projections, depending on the field of view of the panorama. You also learned that for more artistic effects, you can use other projections such as the fisheye or the stereographic. The latter is particularly useful to achieve the nice-looking effect that makes your image resemble a little planet. You also learned how to achieve a similar effect by using Gimp.

Now that you know many things about editing images, in the next chapter, I will show you how to start editing the videos that you take from your camera.

CHAPTER 10

■ ■ ■

Movie Editing

Today, many digital cameras offer the ability to record videos. Some of them even allow you to record in high-definition. This is very handy since you do not need to carry a completely different device for just creating video clips.

By now, you should know that an image can be improved using software in the computer. The same holds true for videos. Because videos are an encoded sequence of images, called frames, once the videos are copied into your computer, you can edit them with some of the same techniques you learned from the past chapters and some new ones. The main difference is that you will need to use different software to achieve that.

The video editing software that I am going to show you in this chapter is called Avidemux. The other leading open-source video-editing package is Blender, which offers more features, but it is much more complicated to use because it is geared towards 3D animation. Avidemux is a condensed name derived from *audio-video multiplexer*. A multiplexer, or mux for short, is the algorithm that compresses all the images into one file. Avidemux allows you to easily create movies, it is cross-platform, and it is free. As with all open-source programs, if you use it and like it, please consider making a small donation to the site and programmers. It offers a lot of functionality that will mostly cover all your video editing needs. If you haven't done so, go to the Appendix to find information about downloading and installing Avidemux.

User Interface

The first thing that you need to do to start creating a movie is to open a video file. A video file can be encoded in many file types, with avi, mpg, and mov being the most common ones. The specific file type that your camera produces will depend on your camera make and model. You can open a video easily by selecting File → Open. You can also drag and drop the video into the Avidemux window from your file browser.

Frame Selection and Playback Options

Avidemux presents an easy-to-use interface (shown in Figure 10-1). The lower part of the screen offers you playback options and frame selection. You can use this to play the video at different speeds, select the current frame, or make a selection of frames for editing.

Figure 10-1. *This image shows the frame selection and playback portion of Avidemux with an AVI-format movie loaded. Note that the coloration and contrast in the preview here may be different than what is actually in the video or will be saved in the video.*

I will now describe the entire interface of the frame selection and playback portion of Avidemux. The current frame of the video, which is the one displayed in the window, is represented by the position of the main horizontal slider, which is shown as about one-quarter of the way through the video clip. In normal playback, it will move from the beginning of the video (left-most position) to the end of the video (right-most position). You can also manually move it to select another frame. The current frame is also represented by the Frame and Time textboxes. You can enter another frame number or time and the current frame will change accordingly.

The buttons in the middle of this portion allow you to control the playback of the video. From left to right, the first two buttons are Play and Stop. They allow you to respectively play or stop the playback. The next two buttons allow you to move frame by frame in reverse or forward motion. The following two buttons give you the ability to move forward or backwards many frames at a time. The next button, pictured with an A, defines the begining of the selection at the current frame. The selection will contain this frame. The following button, pictured with a B, defines the end of the selection at the current frame. The selection will not contain this frame, but the previous one.

You can select a specific part of the video by using the A and B buttons. First, set the current frame to the initial frame of the selection you want. You can do this in a few different ways, such as moving the slider, or inserting a frame number, a specific time, and so forth. After the current frame is set, you need to click the A button. By doing this, the beginning of the selection is set to the current frame. After doing that, you need to set the current frame to the last frame of the selection you want. Then, click on the button that allows you to move one frame forward, which is the fourth from left to right. Now you have to click the B button. This is because B represents the frame after the last frame in the selection. Figure 10-2 shows how the selection is represented as a blue rectangle over the slider.

Figure 10-2. The blue box over the slider shows a selection in Avidemux.

Now that you have a specific part of the video selected, you can cut, copy, or delete it. Just go to the Edit menu and select the proper option. If you cut or copy the selection, you can then paste it in a different location using the same menu.

The next two buttons allow you to search for the next or previous black frame. This is useful when looking for fade outs when changing a scene. The last two buttons allow you to go to the beginning or to the end of the video.

On the right side of this portion of Avidemux, there is a small slider on a gradient background, called a scrubber. It allows you to "scrub" back and forth in your video at a slow speed. This slider allows you to play the video in slow motion at a controlled speed, whether it is forward or backward. Sometimes it is useful to play the video at a slow speed. Instead of clicking the Next or Previous Frame button many times to achieve this effect, you can move this slider slightly to the right or to the left and the video will move with a proportional speed depending on how far you move the red line from the center. There are also two buttons that show the current beginning and end frame numbers of the selection that you have chosen. If you click on any of those two buttons, the current frame will change to the one you clicked.

You can append a new video to the end of the current one by selecting File → Append. Also, you can just drag and drop the video to the Avidemux window. The recently added video will be appended after the end of the current video. Continuing this way, you can create a large video based on small video clips. Note that the videos that you want to append must have the same size and frame rate as the one already open in Avidemux. You may need to crop, resize, or change the frame rate of the videos that you want to append, or the one already open in Avidemux.

Codecs and Video Formats

The left column of Avidemux, highlighted in Figure 10-3, offers you a selection of which video and audio codecs to use. Codec is short for *coder-decoder*. It means that it is software than can code and decode information, such as the sequence of images of a video. In very simple terms, you can think of coding as generating the video, and decoding as playing it. Also, you can select the format of the resulting video.

Figure 10-3. The encoding portion of Avidemux is highlighted.

There are many options for audio and video codecs. One of them is Copy, which just copies the original video without re–encoding, therefore diminishing the video creation time. Another one is Raw, which does not compress each frame, resulting in very large files. There are many different encoders available and you can configure them by selecting one and then clicking on the Configure button. If you are in doubt, I recommend you use the MPEG-4 ASP video codec and the MP3 audio codec.

The format option allows you to specify the format of the resulting video. Some of the formats are AVI (Audio Video Interleave), MPEG (Moving Picture Experts Group), FLV (Flash Video), and MKV (Matroska Multimedia Container). AVI and MPEG are the most common video formats and they support many different codecs. FLV is commonly used for embedded web videos. If you want to encode your file with the FLV format, you will need to select FLV1 codec for video, MP3 codec for audio, and FLV as the video format. Then, click on Audio → Filters, which opens the dialog box shown in Figure 10-4, check Resampling, and set it to 44100.

The MKV format has the goal of becoming the standard format of multimedia content, it is open-source and it is increasing in popularity.

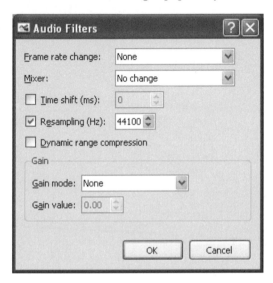

Figure 10-4. This image shows the needed audio configuration for encoding FLV videos in Avidemux.

Frame Rate

A video is a sequence of frames that are shown one after another. Each new frame will appear on the video based on a specific predefined speed. This speed is called *frame rate*. It is measured in frames per second, or *fps*. For example, if your video has a frame rate of 10 fps, it means that the video will show 10 frames every second, or that the video will show the next frame every 0.1 seconds.

There are some standards for video being used around the world. One of these standards is called PAL (*Phase Alternating Line*). This standard uses a frame rate of 25 fps and is being used in most of the countries in Africa, Asia, Europe, and Oceania.

Another standard for video is NTSC (*National Television System Committee*). This standard is being used in most of the countries in North and South America, as well as Japan and some other Asian countries. The frame rate used by this standard is 30 fps.

The cinema and film industry has been using a standard frame rate of 24 fps. If you intend to give your videos a cinematic look, you should start by settings your frame rate to 24 fps.

You can change the frame rate of your video to either adhere to a specific standard or to create faster or slower motions. Just go to Video → Frame Rate. A dialog box will appear (Figure 10-5) allowing you to select a specific frame rate or from a predefined list of frame rates; PAL (25 fps), Film (24 fps), and NTSC (30 fps). To access to the predefined list, you need to uncheck Use custom value.

If you set a slower frame rate, each frame will take longer on screen. This has two consequences; moving objects will appear slower and the movie will last longer. On the other hand, if you increase the frame rate, each frame will appear on screen for less time, producing faster moving objects and shortening the length of the video. Note that if what you want is to maintain the same length in your movie but only change the speed of the movie, you should use the Resample filter that is shown later in this chapter.

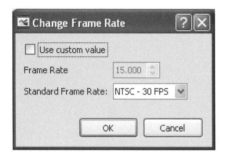

Figure 10-5. *This image shows how to change the frame rate in Avidemux.*

Saving Your Project

Once you have selected the desired audio and video codecs, as well as the format, you can save the final video by selecting File → Save → Save Video. You can also press Ctrl-S for a shortcut access to the Save Video dialog box. Insert the name and location for the video file and press Enter. Make sure that you use the correct file extension so that many media players will recognize the type of file it is and actually play it. For example, if you use an MPEG-4 video, you should use an mpg extension. If there is any error in the combination of codecs and format that you selected, just choose another one and try again. For playback, I recommend you to use the excellent VLC media player, which plays any type of video. This software comes from the open-source project VideoLan.

Now you are able to perform basic operations on video files such as loading, appending, deleting, copying, cutting, pasting, and re-encoding it in a different format. All the movie information—which videos you have appended, which codecs, filters and parameters you have set—form a *project* in Avidemux. You can save the entire project by selecting File → Save Project. Later, you can load the project by selecting Load → Run Project. Note that the individual videos are not stored in the project but only the path to where the files are in your computer.

In the next section, I will show you how to process the video frames using filters.

Filters

As I stated earlier, videos are sequences of images. Therefore, you can edit those images with similar filters that I showed you in previous chapters.

When you use a filter, you will need to re-encode the video. This means that because some, or all, of the frames of the video have been changed, you need to pack them again into a video. Because of this, you need to select a proper video codec before you can access the filters. Below the video label on the left, choose the codec that suits your needs from the drop down menu. This menu has a default value of Copy, which only copies the frames without re-encoding. For using filters, you need to change it to any other codec. If you do not know which one to use, just select MPEG-4 ASP since it gives good general results. After selecting the video codec, you can open the filters dialog box (Figure 10-6) by selecting Video → Filters. Also, you can enter the same menu by clicking on the Filters button under the Video codec settings.

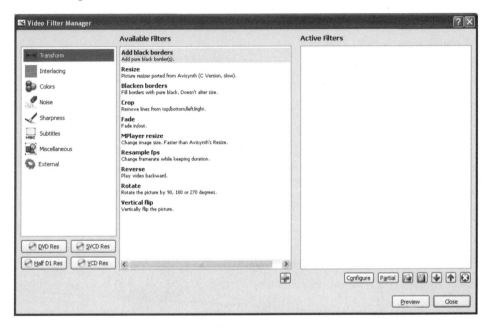

Figure 10-6. The Video Filter Manager dialog box in Avidemux

There are many different types of filters that are available in Avidemux. The first category of filters is called Transform. These filters are similar to the geometric transforms I showed you in Chapter 3, with some others added that are specific to videos.

You can select the category of filters from the left-most part of the dialog box. A list of the effects in that category will appear under the Available Filters section. You can add a filter by just clicking on it and then clicking on the small plus sign below the filters. This will put the filter name in the Active Filters section. There, you can click the Configure button to set the specific properties of that filter. Also, you can click on the Partial button to apply that filter only to a specific set of frames, not the entire video. If you click on the last icon, the small X, you remove that filter.

Transform Filters

The first filter in the Transform section is Add black borders. As its name suggests, this filter gives you the ability to put a black border around the video. This is useful when you want to change the aspect ratio of the movie and you need to "fill in" the missing pixels. Select this filter and press the small green plus (+)

sign at the bottom of the dialog box. Another dialog box will appear asking for the size in pixels of the border that you want to add (Figure 10-7).

I will use the added border to change the aspect ratio of the video from 4:3 to 16:9. The original video has a resolution of 640x480, so I will add 216 pixels of black border to its width; 108 on the left and 108 on the right. This way, I will have a video with a resolution of 856x480, which has an aspect ratio of approximately 16:9. Although a width of 853 would give an aspect ratio closer to 16:9, I recommend that you always use multiples of 8 for both width and height because some codecs have problems with non-standard sizes. Figure 10-8 shows the result of changing the video aspect ratio from 4:3 to 16:9. Note how the black borders increase its width to obtain the new aspect ratio.

Figure 10-7. The Add Borders filter interface. You can set the black border size in pixels.

Figure 10-8. The result of adding a black border to the video in Avidemux to change the aspect ratio of the video from 4:3 to 16:9.

The next filter in this section is called Resize. This filter allows you to change the dimensions of the video. If you uncheck the Lock Aspect Ratio option, you can define any width and any height for the output video. When the Lock Aspect Ratio option is checked, as in Figure 10-9, you can select a specific aspect ratio for resizing, such as 4:3 or 16:9, under Destination to change the output video into that aspect ratio. Also, you can resize the video by using a percent of the original video. Remember to use standard sizes or at least multiples of 8 for width and height because some codecs might have problems with custom sizes. When you change those values, the width and height is calculated automatically. You can even change width or height alone and the other will change accordingly to maintain the same aspect ratio. Figure 10-10 shows the result of resizing the video to half the width and half the height.

There is a Resize Method option that allows you to select which method to use. I suggest that you use the Lanczos method. You can refer to Chapter 3 for more details on this.

Figure 10-9. The resize dialog box in Avidemux

Figure 10-10. The result of resizing the video to half width and half height in Avidemux

There is another useful filter in this list that is called Crop. With this filter, you can reduce the size of the video without altering the shape of the objects or people in the video. It offers an easy-to-use interface (Figure 10-11) in which you can review the entire video and check if you have cropped too much or too little. Note that you can't click and drag the crop like you do in most photo editing programs. You have to use the numeric inputs. There is also an Auto crop button, which is useful when you have a well-defined area to crop, such as black borders. You can see the resulting video in Figure 10-12.

Figure 10-11. The Crop filter dialog box in Avidemux

Figure 10-12. The result of cropping the previous video

There is a very useful filter in this section called Fade. It allows you to fade in or fade out on any selection of frames. This allows you to blend two different clips with a smooth transition from one to the other. Also, you can check the option Fade to black to open or close scenes. The dialog box is shown in Figure 10-13.

Figure 10-13. The Fade filter options dialog box in Avidemux

There is a filter that allows you to rotate the video in 90-, 180-, or 270-degree increments (Figure 10-14). This filter is called Rotate. It is simple and effective; it just moves the pixels so the video quality remains the same.

This filter is useful when the video was taken in a different angle, such as portrait mode, as you can see in the example in Figure 10-15, or when because of some problematic codec the video that you have is rotated.

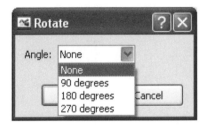

Figure 10-14. The options for the Rotate filter in Avidemux

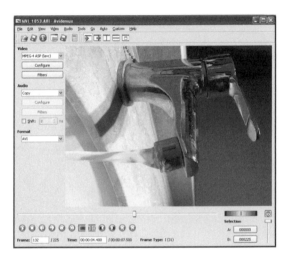

Figure 10-15. This image shows the result of rotating the video by 270 degrees. This is useful for correcting videos taken in portrait mode.

Another simple filter that is available in Avidemux is the Vertical Flip filter. It is similar to the Rotate filter, but it vertically flips the video. Using these two filters together, you can solve all simple orientation problems in your videos.

There are other filters in this section that can be of help. MPlayer resize produces the same result as the Resize filter and it is usually faster. They both have the same interface, which was previously described. The Blacken borders filter did not work on my machine, but it can be easily obtained by just cropping the video and then adding black borders to it.

All the filters in Avidemux are processed from top to bottom, as shown in Figure 10-16, and you can change their order by selecting one of them from the Active Filters list and clicking on the up/down arrows. It will move the selected filter up or down the list, accordingly. You can also change the selected filter configuration by clicking on the Configure button.

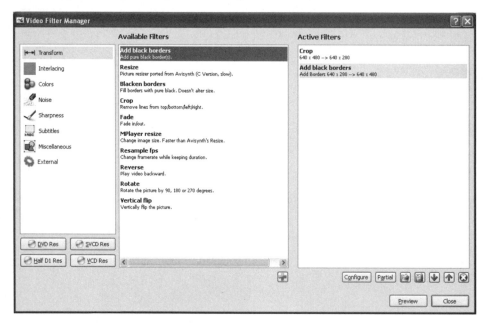

Figure 10-16. You can use more than one active filter to achieve a different result.

The Reverse filter can be helpful to fix videos that are being played backwards, or to add an artistic effect to your movie. Basically, this filter inverts the order of the frames, so the movement in your video will be seen backwards.

You can use the Resample filter to alter the number of frames of the video. The duration of the movie will remain the same. For example, if you resample a video from 30 to 60 fps, Avidemux will duplicate the number of frames so that the video maintains the same duration played at 60 fps. On the other hand, if you change it from 30 to 15 fps, Avidemux will use every other frame to generate the output video.

Color Filters

Another useful section of filters in Avidemux are the Color Filters. In television, the YUV color space has been widely used. It represents how humans perceive color better than the RGB color space, but not as good as the HSV or Lab color spaces. The Y (luma) channel represents light, while the U and V channels represent color components or chromas. Avidemux works with this color space.

You can set the brightness and contrast of the movie by using the Contrast filter under the Color section. When you add the Contrast filter, you will see something similar to Figure 10-17. Just move the brightness and contrast sliders and you will see the effects on the current frame. You can also move the frames slider so that you can preview how the effect will look in other frames. For more details on brightness and contrast, you can refer to Chapter 4.

Figure 10-17. The original image in the brightness and contrast dialog box in Avidemux

You can also change hue and saturation of the video. This is useful for adjusting the colors that you would like to see in the final movie. The hue represents the specific color that you want to define, such as blue, red, and so forth. Saturation represents the intensity of this color, such as bright red or washed blue.

You can access this functionality from the MPlayer Hue filter. MPlayer is the name of another project from which Avidemux took the code for this functionality. This filter is under the Colors category. Once you add this filter, a dialog box like Figure 10-18 will appear. You can set the new hue and saturation of the video by just moving the two sliders in the dialog box. For more details about hue and saturation, please refer to Chapter 4.

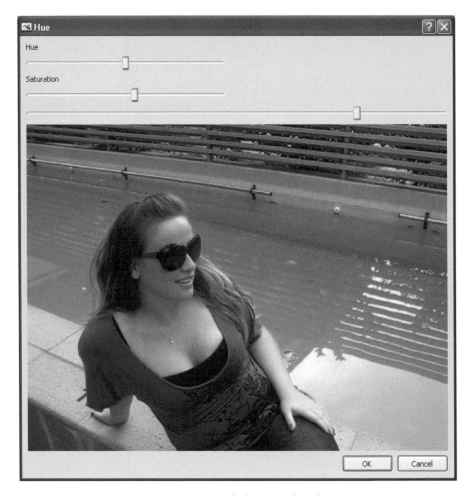

Figure 10-18. This image shows the Hue dialog box of Avidemux..

Some artistic videos are shot in black and white. You can achieve this look in Avidemux easily. Remember that the color space used in Avidemux is YUV, where Y is the luma, which represents the intensity of light, and the other channels represent the color information. If you want to convert your video into grayscale (black and white), you can just keep the luma (Y) channel and discard the others. You can achieve this with the Luma only filter in Avidemux.

More Filters

There are many more filters that you can use depending on the type of video that you are working on. Under the Interlacing section of filters, there are many filters that you can use to remove the interlacing in some videos. Interlacing has been used for transmission of standard television to CRT TVs over the airwaves, and is also used in DVDs for TV. What interlacing is, basically, is that not every single frame is transmitted entirely at once. A frame is divided into odd and even horizontal lines. All odd horizontal lines of the frame are sent and then all even horizontal lines are sent, which combined form the full frame. This is why that type of video is called *interlaced*. If you see an interlaced video on a progressive scan screen, such as an LCD computer display, you will notice some artifacts. You can use these Deinterlacing filters to remove those artifacts.

Under the Noise section, you can find several filters for noise reduction on your video. Median filter is usually good for removing noise, but can generate too much blur. There are many other noise reduction filters that you can try on Avidemux.

You can also increase or decrease the sharpness of your videos. In the Sharpness section in the filters dialog box in Avidemux, you can choose from many sharpening and blurring algorithms. The sharpening algorithms are Asharp, Sharpen, and MSharpen. Asharp is an adaptive sharpening algorithm so it produces good overall results. Sharpen is a simple and fast sharpener. MSharpen allows you to sharpen your video without amplifying noise. You should experiment with those three and see which one gives you the best results.

The blurring algorithms present in Avidemux are Gauss smooth, Mean, Median, MSmooth, and Soften. All of these methods produce a slightly similar blurred video, although MSmooth produces a more pronounced blurred effect. For more details about blurring, sharpening, and noise reduction, please go to Chapter 5.

Under the Miscellaneous section, you can use the Add Framenumber filter to include the number of the frame on the video. This can be useful for reviewing a video so that the frame number is easily seen without any video editing software.

Summary

Today, many digital cameras offer the ability to record videos. Some of them even do so in high definition. In previous chapters, you have learned about many transforms that you can apply to an image. In this chapter, you learned how to apply some of these transforms to a video file. Also, you learned about some extra operations only applicable to a video, such as changing its frame rate, or adding fade outs. You are now able to edit your videos, rotate them, adjust their color, crop, or resize them. Also, you can copy, cut, and paste sections of them as well as append more videos to make a simple movie.

In the previous chapters, I have been discussing many tools and applications that you can use in your computer to enhance your images and videos. For the next chapter, I will cover something different. I will show you an application that works inside your camera, enhancing the way you take your photographs: the Canon Hack Development Kit (CHDK).

■■■

CHAPTER 11

Canon Hack Development Kit

The Cannon Hack Development Kit (CHDK) is software that enhances the features of some Canon cameras. It is the result of excellent work of many people around the world. The web site for the project contains up-to-date information, a forum, downloads, and a wiki page. You can visit it at
http://chdk.wikia.com

This software is not intended to produce permanent changes to your camera, so you can try it and then you can decide if you want to continue using it or not. If you decide not to use it, you can simply delete some files from your camera's flash memory card, put it back into your camera, and it would be like CHDK was never there.

One of the main advantages of using this software is that it enables you to shoot in raw mode on cameras that do not have this option available. Shooting in raw mode is a good choice because it allows you to select the white balance on the computer afterward. Also, the color depth is larger than the processed .jpg file.

Another interesting feature of CHDK is the continuous display of different indicators, such as battery, temperature, histograms, and zebra mode for a visual representation of under-and over-exposed areas in the image.

Exposure time is also enhanced. Using CHDK, you can select from an extremely fast 1/10,000" exposure to a very slow 64" exposure. By using these extreme parameters, you can create a new variety of shots that are impossible to capture on the camera without the use of CHDK. Other parameters, such as aperture, focus, and ISO, are also enhanced.

You can easily use the bracketing technique with CHDK. You can take many continuous pictures by just maintaining the shutter button pressed and the camera automatically will be changing such parameters as exposure time, ISO, or aperture on each capture. By using this feature, you can take the images needed for creating an HDR image.

There are many other additions in CHDK. Some of them even transform your camera into a more versatile device. CHDK allows you to read text files stored on your memory card, display a calendar, and even play games. For example, you can copy tutorials to your camera so that you can read them on-site or play a game while waiting for a specific shot.

For more advanced users, CHDK also has the ability to run scripts. This allows you to write or download programs that add more features to your camera. For example, by using a script, you could add a motion detection feature to your camera so that you can photograph lightning. For programmers, the source code of CHDK is released under the GNU Public License. This gives you full access to the project so that you can compile a customized version that suits your needs.

You can visit http://fiveprime.org/hivemind/Tags/chdk to look at some pictures taken with the extra capabilities of CHDK. On that site, you can also search for other tags, such as the tag qtpfsgui, which will give you HDR-looking images produced with that software.

> ■ **Note** By using CHDK, you may void the Canon warranty and you may damage your camera. This chapter is for advanced users only. If you use CHDK, you're taking a risk with your expensive camera, so keep that in mind.

Installation

First, make sure that you have a Canon PowerShot camera. CHDK only works for those cameras, at least for now. Also, make sure that you have a memory card reader; the USB cable for image transfers will not work. If your computer does not have a built-in memory card reader, don't worry. You can buy a cheap USB memory card reader at any electronics store.

To install CHDK, you need to know your camera model and its firmware version. The firmware is the software that runs inside your camera control it. Finding out the camera model is easy; it should be written on your camera body or you may already know it. To get the firmware version of your camera, you will need to ask your camera directly. Don't worry, I will show you how to do it. You first need to remove the memory card from your camera and put it into the memory card reader. Then, you need to create two files there.

Creating the Files in Microsoft Windows

If you are using Windows, after you insert the memory card into the reader, it should be accessible under *My Computer*. Make a note of the drive letter assigned to this memory card because you are going to need it. In my case, the drive letter assigned by Windows is E:, as shown in Figure 11-1.

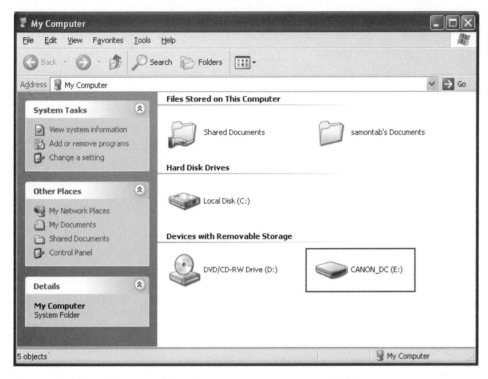

Figure 11-1. The drive letter (E:) assigned to my memory card in Windows.

Now, open the command prompt. On Windows, you can access it by going into the Start menu → All Programs → Accessories → Command Prompt. You can also go to the command prompt by using a shortcut: hold the Windows key on your keyboard and press R, then type cmd and press Enter.

Once you are in the command prompt, you need to go to the drive letter designated to your memory card. In my case, it is E:, but it may be different on your system. Under the command prompt, just type the designated drive, followed by a colon, and press Enter. In my case, I just typed E:.

You will notice that the prompt now changes to the drive letter you typed. Next, you need to create two empty files there, called ver.req and vers.req. To do that, just type the following code:

```
touch ver.req vers.req
```

You should see something similar to Figure 11-2. After you have done this, you can close the command prompt for now by entering exit or by just closing the window.

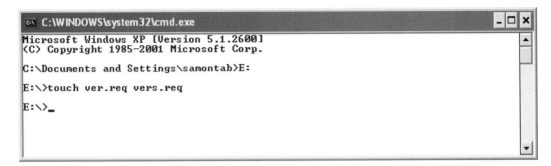

Figure 11-2. This image shows the steps needed to create the files on the memory card in Windows. Note that the drive assigned to your memory card may be different to the one shown here (E:).

Creating the Files in Ubuntu

On Ubuntu, after inserting your memory card into the reader, a desktop icon should appear for the device and it should also be available under your Places tab.

First, open the device by double-clicking the icon in your desktop or selecting it from the Places tab. Now, you need to right-click on any blank area of the top folder. From the pop-up menu, select Create Document → Empty File. Replace the file name new file with ver.req and then repeat the process to create vers.req as another empty file on the flash card. Make sure that you create these two files in the root directory of the device.

If you want to use the terminal to do this, you can just navigate to the root directory of the card and execute the following code:

```
touch ver.req vers.req
```

Asking the Camera for Its Firmware Version

After you create the files, put the memory card back into the camera. While the camera is off, select the playback mode (the one that you use to see the pictures you have made, not the one for taking photos). While in playback mode, turn on the camera. It will not work if you change the mode later, you have to turn the camera on in playback mode. Now, while holding the FUNC/SET button, press the DISP button. The camera should respond with some information, specifically a line saying something like *Firmware Ver GM1.00B*. The part after GM is the firmware version number. In this case, for example, it is *1.00B*.

Okay, so now you have your camera model and its firmware version number. The next step is to get the latest version of CHDK for your camera's specific model and firmware. You can download CHDK from the Download section of the project web site, http://chdk.wikia.com, which leads you to http://mighty-hoernsche.de. Remember that if these pages' locations change in the future, you can always do a web search to find them. On the download page, for each supported camera model and firmware, you will see two zip files: complete and small . Download the complete file as it includes grids, example scripts, additional languages, and so forth. The small file only contains the core of CHDK. Make sure that you download the correct version for your camera model and firmware.

The next step is to unzip the zip file you just downloaded. You will see a CHDK folder, along with the following files: changelog.txt, DISKBOOT.BIN, PS.FIR, readme.txt, and vers.req. Note that different versions or camera models may have slightly different files. Now you need to copy all those files and the

CHDK folder to the root directory of your memory card. Take the memory card out of your camera and use a memory card reader. It does not matter if you have other files on your memory card; the only important thing is that you copy all of these files into the root (top) directory of the card.

Now put the memory card back into the camera. While the camera is off, select the playback mode, as you did last time.

Next, turn your camera on. Press the Menu button and go to the last option, Firm Update. Press the FUNC/SET button to enter. A dialog box will appear asking if you want to update the firmware version. Move to the right and press the FUNC/SET button to accept the update of the firmware version. After doing this, you should see a splash screen indicating the version and date of the software. This means that CHDK is now activated on your camera. If you go to the shooting mode, you will see some extra displays, such as the battery status, the optical temperature, and the time.

Once CHDK is activated, a new mode will be available on your camera: the Alternative (<ALT>) mode. This mode allows you to access the CHDK menu, edit your settings, and run scripts.

You can enter the <ALT> mode by pressing a specific button on your camera. For most cameras, including the A series and the SD or IXUS series, this button is the *Direct Print* button. For a few other cameras, such as the S2 or S3, this button is the *Shortcut* button. You can visit the CHDK project web site for more up-to-date information about this. Pressing this button will toggle the mode, from normal to <ALT>. The display should toggle the word <ALT> at the bottom when the button is pressed. This indicates whether you are in the <ALT> mode or not.

While in <ALT> mode, press the Menu button. This will display the CHDK main menu, as shown in Figure 11-3.

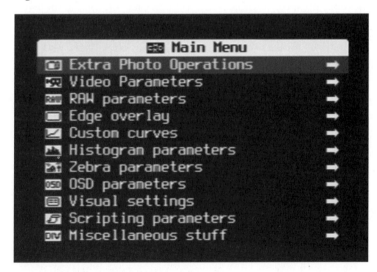

Figure 11-3. The main menu of CHDK

I will first give you an overview of this menu and then I will go into the details of some of the most useful features.

Using the Extra Photo Operations menu, you can access to the enhanced ranges of exposure time, aperture, ISO, and focus (subject distance). Also, you can configure the bracketing settings, among other parameters. For more information about exposure in general, please refer to Chapter 1.

The Video Parameters menu allows you to change many settings for video capture. For example, you can enable optical zoom while recording a video, which is not possible without CHDK. Also, you can set the video quality and the refresh rate, among other things.

The RAW menu allows you to activate or deactivate the saving of raw images along with the JPG files in your camera. Also, it allows you to set different options regarding RAW. You can read more about RAW in Chapter 7.

The Edge overlay menu allows you to activate or deactivate the edge overlay feature, among other specific parameters. When this feature is active, you will see the edges of the current image in the LCD screen when you press or half press the shutter button. This can be useful for taking the images for a panorama or when creating a stop-motion animation because you will know where the objects were positioned in the previous image thanks to the edge overlay. For more information about how to create panoramas, please refer to Chapter 9.

The Custom curves menu allows you to set any predefined curve, such as +1EV, +2EV, or Auto DR, which automatically tries to minimize the under- and over-exposed areas. You can read more about curves in Chapter 4.

Using the Histogram menu, you can select whether or not you want to see a live histogram. You can change the settings of the displayed histogram so that it displays exactly what you need. Chapter 4 explains what a histogram is.

The Zebra menu allows you activate or deactivate the Zebra function. The Zebra mode allows you to see which areas of the image are under- or over-exposed by painting selectable patterns, such as a solid color, blinking colors, or stripes. You can set the sensitivity of under- and over-exposed areas, from 0, which is the least sensible (off), to 32, which is the most sensible. I recommend that you use the value of 1 in each case. When Zebra is activated, you can access this mode by just half pressing the shutter button when taking a photograph.

The OSD menu allows you to change settings for the on screen-display of the CHDK. You can change positioning and select which items you want to be shown on the screen using the OSD layout editor.

The Visual settings menu allows you to change the general appearance of CHDK. This means that you can change the fonts, colors, sizes, and similar properties.

Using the Scripting menu, you can load scripts and select their parameters. At the end of this chapter, I will cover how to load and run scripts.

The Miscellaneous menu allows you to access extra functionality of CHDK. This functionalities range from utilities or games to information about the CHDK builds. Also, it allows you to enable a very nice feature: automatic loading of CHDK. In general, every time you turn your camera off, CHDK will go away. This means that every time you turn your camera on, you will need to enable CHDK by updating the firmware. After some time, this may become tedious. To solve that, just go to the Miscellaneous menu and select the *Make card bootable* option. You won't see any dialog box or change, maybe just a small flash, but that's okay. After doing this, turn your camera off, then take your memory card out and lock it. You can do that by moving the small slider on the side of the card. Now put the memory card back into the camera and you will see that CHDK is automatically loaded. If you want to remove this feature, just unlock the card and turn your camera on. Everything will be the same as before.

Now that you have an overview of CHDK, I will show you step-by-step how to achieve specific tasks that are very useful using this software.

Shooting in RAW

The first thing that you may want to do is to enable the Save RAW option under the RAW menu, as shown in Figure 11-4.

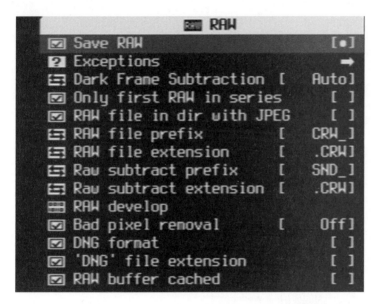

Figure 11-4. Enabling the Save RAW functionality in CHDK

If the Save RAW option is enabled, the camera will copy a RAW file as well as the regular JPG file whenever you shoot an image. Note that this will take longer and consume more space on your memory card. By default, the RAW image will be copied into a folder separate from the JPG files. You can enable the *RAW file in dir with JPEG* option to have all your RAW and JPG files saved to the same directory.

You can open the resulting CRW file with the UFRaw program, which I introduced in Chapter 7. You may notice that the metadata is not present in this file. If you are not sure about what metadata is, please refer to Chapter 6. To obtain the metadata, you can copy it from the JPG file, or you can generate a DNG (Digital Negative) format instead, which is also raw data but preserves the metadata and is compatible with more software. To generate a DNG file, you need to activate the *DNG format* and the *'DNG' file extension* options from the menu shown in Figure 11-4.

When you take a photograph, now an extra DNG file will be created instead of a CRW.

You may need to run a specific script before you are able to start using the DNG format. This is because the script creates some files needed by the DNG procedure. This script is called *badpixel.lua* and it is located in the Test directory. Don't worry about it for now, I will show you how to run this and other scripts later in this chapter.

Using Zebra Mode

Zebra mode allows you to see which portions of the image will turn out to be under-and over-exposed if you take a photograph with your current settings. This mode can be very helpful when taking multiple images for later HDRI-compilation, as discussed in Chapter 7. After enabling it, you can access the Zebra mode by just half pressing the shutter button. Areas that are under- or over-exposed with the current settings will be marked in the LCD screen with a solid red color. Once you have determined that an area is going to be over-exposed, for example, you could change the controls in your camera so that less light is captured, generating a better exposure. Refer to Chapter 1 for more information about proper exposure and how to use your camera controls.

To enable Zebra mode, just go to the Zebra menu and activate the Draw Zebra option (see Figure 11-5). I normally recommend using Solid as the Zebra mode, but you can change it to your liking. It is important that you set both thresholds to 1 so that a small under-or over-exposure is captured, as shown in Figure 11-6.

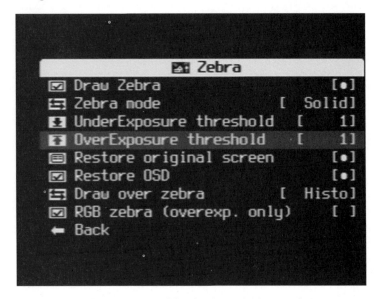

Figure 11-5. The settings used for displaying Zebra mode in CHDK

Figure 11-6. *This image shows an example of the Zebra mode. This image seen in the LCD screen when the shutter button is half pressed shows a large overexposed portion due to the bright light marked in a solid color. Also, there is a small area underexposed on the left, also marked by the Zebra mode.*

Displaying Grids

As I discussed in Chapter 1, image composition is important to taking a compelling shot. CHDK enables you to show different grids that help you align your composition. These grids are lines or shapes that are present all the time on the screen display. This is very useful for composing because you can set a grid that represents the rule of thirds, for example. This means that you do not have to guess the position of these lines; you can actually see them on the screen while composing. CHDK allows you to select among several grids and you can put even more if you want. To select a grid, you first need to go to the *OSD parameters* menu. Once you are there, you need to enter into the *Grid* menu.

Once you are on the *Grid* menu (Figure 11-7), you need to activate the *Show grid lines* option.

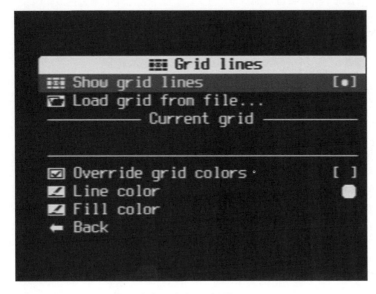

Figure 11-7. Activating the grids in CHDK

You are now ready to load any type of grid that is currently on the memory card. You can read more about composition rules and grids in Chapter 1. Open a grid by selecting the *Load grid from file* option. A dialog box will appear showing you all the grids present on the memory card. You can explore all of them and see which one fits your needs. For example, 3to2grid shows how much of the image will be visible when cropped to fit a 3:2 aspect ratio. Other grids show different things, such third_h and third_v, which are based on the rule of thirds.

CHDK comes with some example grid lines, but you can add more if you want. These grids are stored under the GRIDS folder inside the CHDK folder of the memory card. Just putting new grids in that folder allows you to use them. There is also a readme.txt file with instructions on how to build your own grids.

Changing the Exposure time

With CHDK, you have an increased range of exposure time. You can access this feature by going into the *Extra Photo Operations* menu and changing the *Override shutter speed* and *Value factor* options. The *Override shutter speed* option allows you to select the exposure time in seconds. The *Value factor* option allows you to turn this feature on or off. To select the maximum exposure time available, which is 64 seconds, you need to set the *Override shutter speed* option to 64 and *Value factor* to 1 (see Figure 11-8). The minimum exposure time available is 1/10,000[th] of a second, which allows you to photograph very fast subjects such as moving birds or insects on a sunny day.

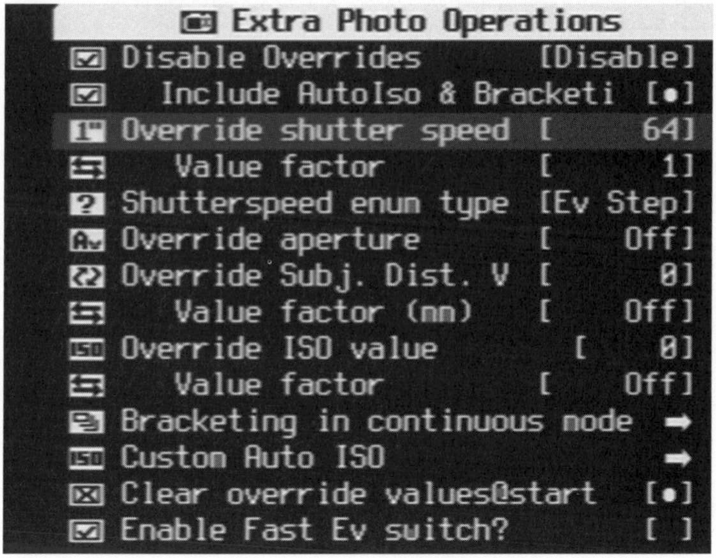

```
       Extra Photo Operations
  ☑ Disable Overrides       [Disable]
  ☑    Include AutoIso & Bracketi  [●]
  ▮  Override shutter speed  [     64]
  ⛶      Value factor        [      1]
  ❷  Shutterspeed enum type  [Ev Step]
  Av  Override aperture       [    Off]
  ↩  Override Subj. Dist. V  [      0]
  ⛶      Value factor (mn)   [    Off]
  ISO  Override ISO value      [      0]
  ⛶      Value factor        [    Off]
  ▣  Bracketing in continuous mode  ➡
  ISO  Custom Auto ISO                ➡
  ☒  Clear override values@start  [●]
  ☑  Enable Fast Ev switch?   [  ]
```

Figure 11-8. Setting the maximum exposure time available in CHDK

Bracketing mode

Using this mode, you can get the images needed to create an HDR image, discussed in Chapter 7. While you keep the shutter button pressed, the camera will change the exposure parameters automatically and continue shooting different images. You can release the shutter button when you have taken enough photographs.

To activate this mode, first you need to activate the continuous mode on your camera. This is the mode you use to take several images while maintaining the shutter button pressed. Consult your camera manual on how to achieve this because every model is different. After doing that, you need to go to the *Extra Photo Operations* menu and select *Bracketing in continuous mode* (see Figure 11-9).

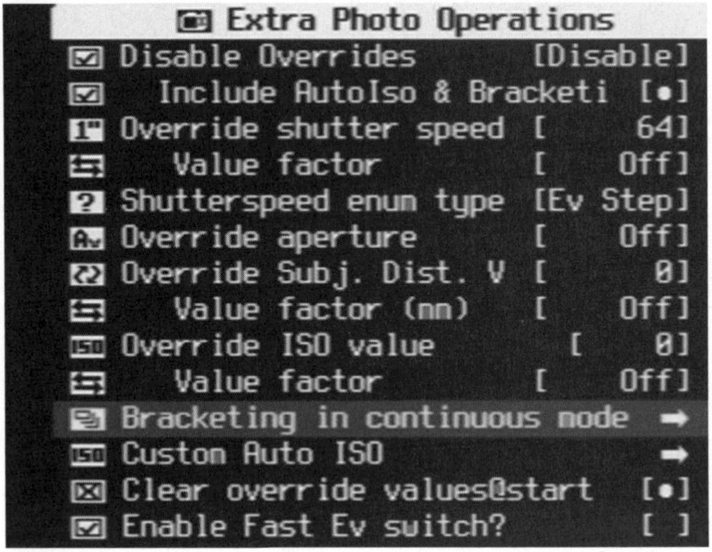

Figure 11-9. Accessing the bracketing mode in CHDK

Using the *Bracketing in continuous mode* menu (Figure 11-10), you can select which control you want to change: Exposure time, Aperture, Focus, or ISO. The most recommended setting for creating HDR images is bracketing in exposure time. You can select how much the camera will change the exposure from one photograph to the other. In this case, I used 2 Ev or full stops. This means that the first photograph will be taken with your defined settings, the next one will have +2 Ev, the following -2 Ev. After that, the next photograph will have +4 Ev, then -4 Ev, and so on until you release the shutter button. This is due to the *Bracketing type* selected, +/-, which means that it will first add and then subtract the selected value, alternately, for each new photograph taken.

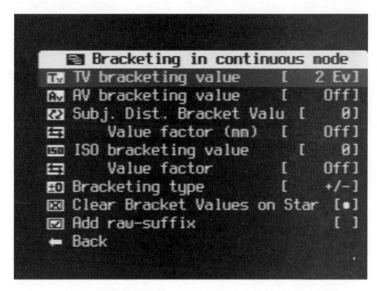

Figure 11-10. An example value for exposure time bracketing

Figure 11-11 shows one example of using this feature. I used CHDK to take three consecutive shots while changing the exposure time by two full stops on each one. Then, I used HDR imaging techniques to merge these three images into one, shown in Figure 11-12.

Figure 11-11. This image shows three consecutive images taken with exposure time bracketing.

Figure 11-12. This image shows the resulting image after processing the previous images with HDR imaging techniques. Go to Chapter 7 for more information about HDR imaging.

Games and More

CHDK includes some applications such as games, a calendar, and a text file reader. You can access them by going into the *Miscellaneous* menu and then selecting the application you want to access.

You can access games by going into *Miscellaneous* and selecting *Games*, as shown in Figure 11-13. There are four games available in CHDK, which you can see in Figure 11-14.

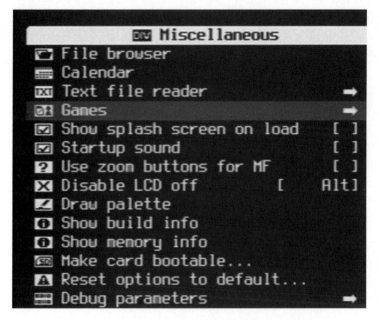

Figure 11-13. This image shows how to access games in CHDK.

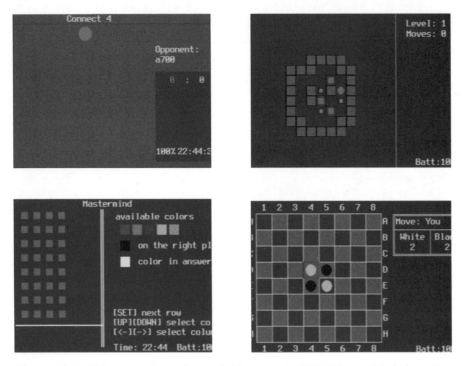

Figure 11-14. This image shows the available games in CHDK: Reversi, Sokoban, Connect 4 and Mastermind.

You can access the Calendar by going into the *Miscellaneous* menu and selecting *Calendar*. You will see something similar to Figure 11-15. You can change the month by moving left or right and the year by moving up or down.

Figure 11-15. This image shows the Calendar in CHDK. Use left or right to change the month and up or down for the year.

The Text file reader can be useful for reading photography tutorials or any type of instructions on-site. You can access this application by going into the *Miscellaneous* menu and selecting *Text file reader*, as shown in Figure 11-16. After that, you have to load a text file and you will be able to read it on the LCD screen. To add your own text file, just put the memory card into the computer, open the CHDK folder, and go to the BOOKS folder. Inside you will see a sample readme.txt file. Any text file that you put into that folder will be readable later in your camera with this tool, as shown in Figure 11-17.

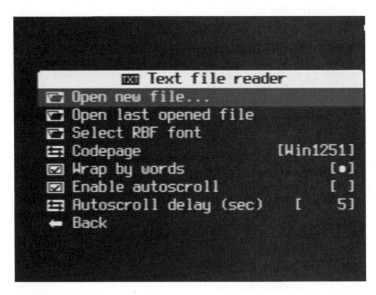

Figure 11-16. This image shows the Text file reader menu in CHDK.

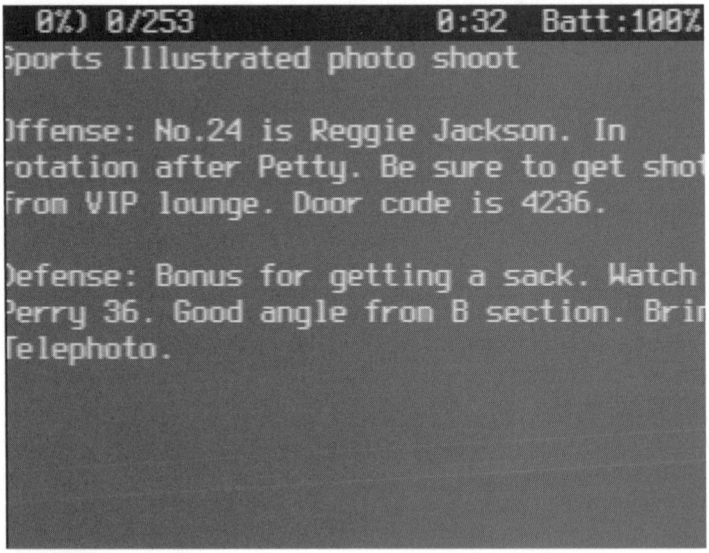

Figure 11-17. This image shows a text file being read in CHDK.

Running Scripts

A script is a set of instructions for your camera. With them, you can make your camera automatically do almost anything you can do with it manually. One example of a very basic script is the autoshutter functionality. In a script, you can say to the camera to wait for 10 seconds and then shoot the picture. The nice thing about scripts is that you can adjust almost any control in the camera, so for example, you could use a script to take three shots with different exposure times or with different zoom levels. All you have to do is press the shutter button and the camera will execute the script, or set of instructions, automatically. This has a lot of benefits. For example, when taking multiple shots, you only press the shutter button the first time so it will not move for the rest of the shots. If you plan to take bracketing shots, you don't need to manually change the settings for each photo; the camera will take care of it automatically.

To run a script, first you need to load it. Go to the *Scripting parameters* menu and then select the *Load script from file* option (Figure 11-18).

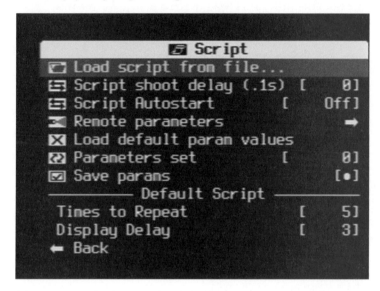

Figure 11-18. The Script menu in CHDK.

You will see a default.bas script and two folders: EXAMPLES and TEST, as shown in Figure 11-19. These are the files that are in the SCRIPTS folder under CHDK on the memory card. If you want to add new scripts, just copy them to that folder. You can write scripts in two different scripting languages: basic (.bas) and lua (.lua). Teaching you these two programming languages is beyond the scope of this book, but Google is your friend.

The default.bas script is the one loaded by default and it does nothing. Because the system always needs one script to be loaded, when you don't want to use any scripts, you should select this one. The EXAMPLES folder contains simple scripts. They have simple functionality, such as reading from the keys you press and printing on the screen, as well as waiting for a specific number of seconds. The TEST folder contains scripts that you can use to test if the system is okay. There is one script in the TEST folder that you should run if you want to use the DNG functionality. It is the badpixel.lua script.

Once you load one script, you can set its parameters. Pressing the shutter button is how you start running a script, just like shooting a photograph. If you are in <ALT> mode, you will start running the loaded script. On the other hand, if you are in the normal mode, you will shoot the photograph. Note that you can also press the shutter button to interrupt a script.

For example, if you select the countdown.lua script from the EXAMPLES folder, three parameters will appear at the bottom of the screen: hours, minutes, and seconds. You can set these three parameters with the left or right buttons. Once you are done, press Menu to close the dialog. Make sure that you are still in <ALT> mode and then press the shutter button. This will print the word STARTED in the screen and will ask you to press the SET button to begin. Once you press the SET button, the countdown begins. Once it is finished, it tells you to press Menu to stop. When you press Menu, the script stops and the word FINISHED appears.

Let's see another example. Load the metronome.lua script and set the beats/min to any value that you want. Then, press Menu to exit the dialog box and while in <ALT> mode, press the shutter button. It will ask you to press the SET button to begin. Once you press that button, the LED of your camera should blink at the specified rate. Press Menu to exit this script. You can also interrupt it at any time by pressing the shutter button again.

Now let's run the badpixel.lua script from the TEST folder, since it is required to use the DNG format. This script tests how many bad pixels are in your camera. To open this script, you need to go inside the TEST directory (Figure 11-19).

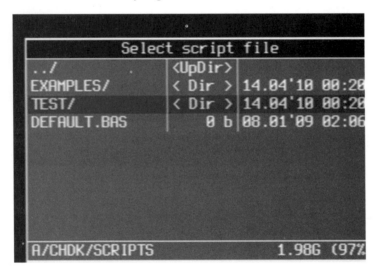

Figure 11-19. This image shows the included scripts in CHDK.

Now you need to select the badpixel.lua script, which should be the first one in the list, as shown in Figure 11-20.

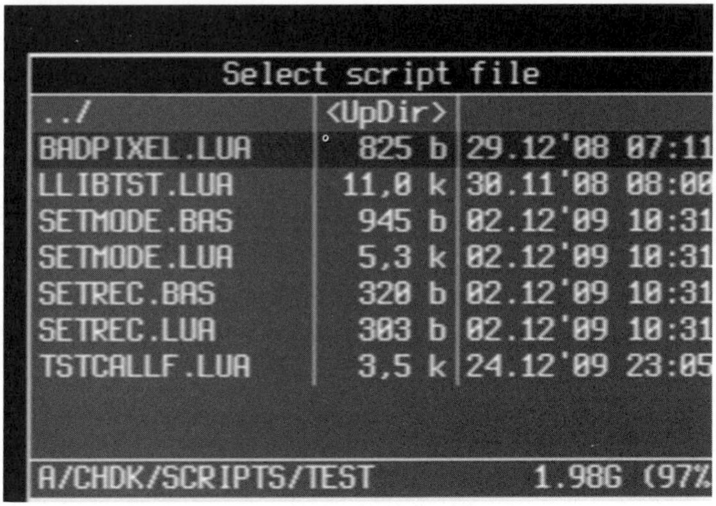

```
                    Select script file
../                      <UpDir>
BADPIXEL.LUA          °   825 b   29.12'08 07:11
LLIBTST.LUA            11,0 k     30.11'08 08:00
SETMODE.BAS              945 b    02.12'09 10:31
SETMODE.LUA             5,3 k     02.12'09 10:31
SETREC.BAS              320 b     02.12'09 10:31
SETREC.LUA              303 b     02.12'09 10:31
TSTCALLF.LUA            3,5 k     24.12'09 23:05


A/CHDK/SCRIPTS/TEST            1.98G (97%
```

Figure 11-20. Selecting the script to be loaded

Now you are ready to execute the loaded script. Close the dialog box by pressing the Menu key. Now, change your camera mode into the shooting mode, the one you normally use to take photographs, and while in <ALT> mode press the shutter button. This will execute the script. It should take a while and the script will take a couple of photographs. Don't worry. Once it is finished, press SET to save the results. Now you can exit <ALT> mode and continue using your camera normally.

You can explore the other scripts as well and even download more from the CHDK web site. Note that there isn't an organized repository for scripts and sometimes instead of just downloading a file, you may have to copy and paste the text of the script from the web page into a text file and save it yourself with the correct extension (.bas or .lua).

At http://chdk.wikia.com/wiki/UBASIC/Scripts, you can find some basic (.bas) scripts. I suggest that you try at least the motion-detection script (Fast Motion detection). It will automatically take pictures when something in the scene moves.

At http://chdk.wikia.com/wiki/LUA, you can access to Lua (.lua) scripts. The Lua scripting language is rather new in the CHDK community, but it allows you to create more advanced features than basic scripts, such as accessing the files on your memory card.

Remember that for the camera to recognize the scripts, you have to put the script files into the SCRIPTS folder under CHDK on the memory card. Also, remember to name the script file properly, with a .lua or .bas extension, depending on the language in which it was written. Note that some of the scripts are for specific camera models only.

After gaining some experience, you can also even start writing your own scripts, while some of the most advanced readers may compile their own version of CHDK for maximum control. In either case, I recommend that you share your efforts with the community.

Summary

In this chapter, you learned how to install and use the CHDK. With this tool, you can enhance the functionality of your Canon camera. You can now shoot in RAW mode using your point-and-shoot camera. You now have an increased range of exposure time, aperture, and ISO settings. You can easily shoot the needed images to create HDR images using the bracketing mode. You can also avoid shooting under- or over-exposed photographs thanks to the Zebra mode. In addition, you can use your camera to play games, look at a calendar, or read text files. Also, you now can have several grids, the battery level, as well as other indicators, always on your LCD screen.

At the end of this chapter, you learned how to load and run scripts, which further enhance the features that your camera can offer. With scripts, you can detect motion and shoot when something has moved in the scene, for example, which can be useful for capturing lightning or even for security.

I hope this book has helped you get the most out of your camera and not only take better pictures, but construct a powerful yet inexpensive digital darkroom to produce amazing photographs.

Installing the Tools

In this appendix, I will show you how to install the tools used throughout the book. All these programs are freely available for at least Microsoft Windows and Ubuntu.

GIMP

GIMP is a powerful image editor. It is one of the main tools used in this book. The version used in this book is 2.6.7. Installing it is really easy.

Installing GIMP in Microsoft Windows

To install GIMP in Microsoft Windows, you need to download the latest release at `http://www.gimp.org/`, double-click on the downloaded file, and follow the installer instructions.

Installing GIMP in Ubuntu

In Ubuntu, GIMP may be already installed. If for some reason it is not installed, you can always install it by running the following command in the terminal window:

```
sudo apt-get install gimp
```

UFRaw

UFRaw allows you to open RAW images. You can also adjust color balance and many other advanced options. The version used in this book is 0.15.

Make sure that you install GIMP before you install UFRaw. This will allow you to send the converted RAW images directly from UFRaw to GIMP. Also, there are some files that UFRaw needs that come with GIMP.

Installing UFRaw in Microsoft Windows

You can install UFRaw in Microsoft Windows by downloading the latest binaries from the Download and Install section of `http://ufraw.sourceforge.net/`. After that, you need to double-click on the downloaded file and follow the instructions.

Installing UFRaw in Ubuntu

In Ubuntu, you can easily install UFRaw installed by running the following command in the terminal window:

```
sudo apt-get install ufraw
```

Resyntheziser

Resyntheziser is a plug-in for GIMP. This means that you need to have GIMP installed before you install this program. This plug-in has a bug so I will show you how to install it first and then how to patch it to make it work correctly.

Installing Resyntheziser in Microsoft Windows

The first thing that you have to do is to download the zip file of the original resyntheziser plug-in from the following address:

```
http://registry.gimp.org/node/9148.
```

Close GIMP if you have it open. Now we are going to install this plug-in.

You need to make sure that you are able to see hidden files and folders. This is done slightly different between Windows XP and newer versions, such as Vista and 7.

If you are working in Windows XP, first open any folder. Then, in that folder menu, go to Tools → Folder options. There, click on the View tab and click the *Show hidden files and folders* option, as shown in Figure A-1. Click on OK and you are done.

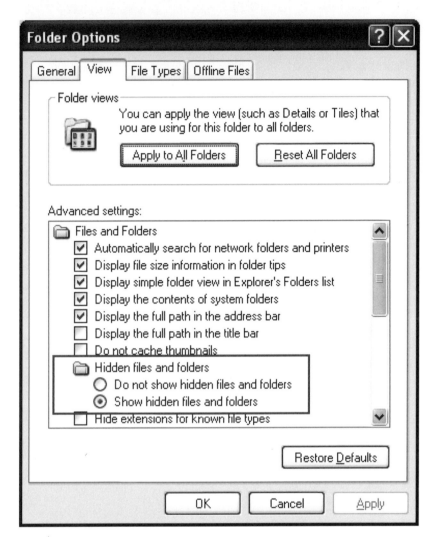

Figure A-1. This image shows how to view hidden files and folders in Windows XP.

If you are working on Windows Vista or 7, the instructions are similar. First, go to the Control Panel and click on Appearance and Personalization. There, under Folder Options, click on *Show hidden files and folders.* This will bring a dialog box similar to Figure A-1. Just select *Show hidden files, folders, and drives* under *Hidden files and folders* and click OK.

Now you need to locate your user folder in GIMP. This location is different between Windows XP and newer versions of Windows, such as Vista and 7.

If you are using Windows XP, the location of this folder is:

```
C:\Documents and Settings\USERNAME\.gimp-VERSION
```

Note that USERNAME is your actual user name and VERSION is the actual version of GIMP. As an example, the location of my user folder of GIMP in Windows XP is C:\Documents and Settings\samontab\.gimp-2.6.

If you are using Windows Vista or 7, the location of this folder is slightly different. It is stored in:

C:\Users\USERNAME\.gimp-VERSION

Note that here as well, USERNAME and VERSION are related to your specific values. In my case, if using Windows 7, the location would be C:\Users\samontab\.gimp-2.6.

The next step is to go into the user folder of GIMP. There, you will see many folders. There are two that are particularly useful: scripts and plug-ins. Any script or plug-in that is added in those respective folders will be installed in GIMP. That is exactly what we are going to do now.

Resynthesizer version 0.16 comes as a compressed file. After you decompress this file, two directories will appear: plug-ins and scripts. You need to copy the contents of these folders into the respective folders of the GIMP user folder. Specifically, you will be copying smart-enlarge.scm and smart-remove.scm into the scripts folder and resynth.exe into the plug-ins folder.

Now, we are going to apply the patch that solves some bug issues. First, download it from http://registry.gimp.org/node/15118. It is a single file called smart-remove.scm. Move this file into the scripts directory of the GIMP user folder, overwriting the previous file.

After doing that, restart GIMP. Plug-ins will be activated. Now you can access this plug-in under the following menu: Filters → Enhance → Heal Selection.

Installing Resyntheziser in Ubuntu

To install Resynthezier in Ubuntu, you need to execute the following command:

sudo apt-get install gimp-resynthesizer

After doing that, you need to download the patch from http://registry.gimp.org/node/15118 and copy it into the GIMP scripts folder, overwriting the previous one. This folder is located at /usr/share/gimp/2.0/scripts. After doing that, restart GIMP. Plug-ins will be activated. Now you can access this plug-in under the following menu: Filters → Enhance → Heal Selection.

Imagemagick

Imagemagick is a powerful command-line utility for image processing. The version used in this book is 6.5.6-10 2009-10-08 Q16.

Installing Imagemagick in Microsoft Windows

To install Imagemagick in Microsoft Windows, you need to go to the Binary Release–Windows section at http://www.imagemagick.org. Download the file that suits your needs. If you do not know which one to download, choose the first option. After doing that, just double-click the downloaded file and follow the instructions.

Installing Imagemagick in Ubuntu

To install Imagemagick in Ubuntu, you only need to execute the following command in the command line:

```
sudo apt-get install imagemagick
```

Hugin

Hugin provides an easy-to-use interface for stitching panoramas and more.

This software is provided for non-commercial use only. The University of British Columbia has applied for a patent on the SIFT algorithm in the United States. Commercial applications of this software may require a license from the University of British Columbia.

The version used in this book is 0.70 because in newer versions, you need to install the automatic control points generators separately, which may be difficult for some people.

Installing Hugin in Microsoft Windows

You can install this version by going to `http://sourceforge.net/projects/hugin/files` and downloading the `hugin-0.7.0_win32-setup.exe` file under the `hugin-0.7.0` directory. After doing that, double-click the file and follow the instructions.

Installing Hugin in Ubuntu

To install Hugin in Ubuntu, you only need to execute the following command in the command line:

```
sudo apt-get install hugin
```

Qtpfsgui

Version 1.8.12 of Qtpfsgui is used in this book, although newer versions are available. At the time of publication, the latest stable version was 1.9.3, but it presented some issues in the implementation of a tone mapping operator, specifically the Durand operator. Because of this, I decided to use a slightly older version that still had the correct implementation of all the tone mapping operators. Also, note that starting from release 2.0, this software will be renamed to Luminance HDR.

Installing Qtpfsgui in Microsoft Windows

For Windows-based systems, you can download version 1.8.12 of Qtpfsgui from the SourceForge download page. Just go to `http://sourceforge.net/projects/qtpfsgui/files/` and select the `qtpfsgui` folder. Inside that folder, choose version 1.8.12. Finally, download the file called `QtpfsguiSetup.exe`. You can access this file directly by going to this location:

```
http://sourceforge.net/projects/qtpfsgui/files/qtpfsgui/1.8.12/QtpfsguiSetup.exe/download
```

After the file has downloaded, double-click it and proceed with the installation.

Installing Qtpfsgui in Ubuntu

For Linux-based systems like Ubuntu, go to `http://sourceforge.net/projects/qtpfsgui/files/` and select the qtpfsgui folder, followed by the 1.8.12 option. There, you need to select the `qtpfsgui-1.8.12.tar.gz` file to download. You can access this file directly from this location:

```
http://sourceforge.net/projects/qtpfsgui/files/qtpfsgui/1.8.12/↵
qtpfsgui-1.8.12.tar.gz/download
```

Extract the files and follow the instructions for installing Qtpfsgui.

Ubuntu users can install the latest repository version by executing the following code in the command line:

```
sudo apt-get install qtpfsgui
```

Avidemux

Avidemux is video editing software. It is simple to use and offers the most common video operations needed for making a short movie or video using the clips from your camera.

Installing Avidemux in Microsoft Windows

To install Avidemux in Microsoft Windows, you need to go to `http://fixounet.free.fr/avidemux` and download the latest release for Microsoft Windows in the Downloads menu. Once the file is downloaded, double-click it and follow the instructions.

Installing Avidemux in Ubuntu

To install Avidemux in Ubuntu, you need to execute the following command under the command line:

```
sudo apt-get install avidemux
```

ExifTool

Phil Harvey created an excellent program called ExifTool. This software allows you to read and write metadata of many types of files, especially image files.

Installing ExifTool in Microsoft Windows

You can install ExifTool in Microsoft Windows by first downloading the Windows executable at `http://www.sno.phy.queensu.ca/~phil/exiftool/`. After you download the file, extract it and you will see a file called `exiftool(-k).exe`. Rename it to `exiftool.exe`. Finally, copy that file into the `c:\windows` folder.

Installing ExifTool in Ubuntu

To install ExifTool in Ubuntu, you need to execute the following command in the command line:

```
sudo apt-get install libimage-exiftool-perl
```

Index

You Need the Companion eBook

Your purchase of this book entitles you to buy the companion PDF-version eBook for only $10. Take the weightless companion with you anywhere.

We believe this Apress title will prove so indispensable that you'll want to carry it with you everywhere, which is why we are offering the companion eBook (in PDF format) for $10 to customers who purchase this book now. Convenient and fully searchable, the PDF version of any content-rich, page-heavy Apress book makes a valuable addition to your programming library. You can easily find and copy code—or perform examples by quickly toggling between instructions and the application. Even simultaneously tackling a donut, diet soda, and complex code becomes simplified with hands-free eBooks!

Once you purchase your book, getting the $10 companion eBook is simple:

❶ Visit **www.apress.com/promo/tendollars/**.

❷ Complete a basic registration form to receive a randomly generated question about this title.

❸ Answer the question correctly in 60 seconds, and you will receive a promotional code to redeem for the $10.00 eBook.

eBookshop

233 Spring Street, New York, NY 10013

3 1901 04492 1585